TRIANGLEPAINT

sherlee
lantz

TRIANGLEPAINT

the viking press
a studio book
new york

Opposite: The Trianglepoint Stitch. All designs in the book are worked in this simple construction.

To

Library of Congress Cataloging in Publication Data

Lantz, Sherlee.
  Trianglepoint.
  (A Studio book)
  Bibliography: p.
  Includes index.
  1. Canvas embroidery—Patterns.   I. Title.
TT778.C3L35   746.4′4   76-3550
ISBN 0-670-73030-0

PHOTOGRAPHY by William F. Pons

ACKNOWLEDGMENTS

I am very grateful to Barbara Burn, editor, and Chris Holme, designer, for their fine work on behalf of this book.

Grazyna Bergman and Martina D'Alton gave time and effort to various phases of manuscript preparation. They have, and deserve, my deepest appreciation and thanks.

I am much indebted to Manuel Keene, of the Metropolitan Museum of Art's Islamic Department, for his indispensable and generous assistance with early Roman mosaic designs.

My young and esteemed friend Léonie Agnew stitched many of the designs. Her intelligent assistance, fastidious work, and care are woven into the book.

For permission to reproduce the following illustrations, I am grateful to:

Dover Publications for the photograph from *Snow Crystals* by W. A. Bentley and W. J. Humphreys (p. 10)

New York Public Library for drawing of honeybee constructions from the *Biblia Naturae* by Jan Swammerdam, 1738 (p. 15)

Metropolitan Museum of Art for "King Khusrau Seated Upon His Throne," from the sixteenth-century Persian manuscript *The Khamasa of Nizami* (p. 16)

Chester Beatty Museum Library, Dublin, for "Iskandar in a Magic Garden," from the fifteenth-century Persian manuscript *An Anthology* (p. 17)

New-York Historical Society for the geometric star pieced quilt (p. 18)

American Museum in Britain, Bath, for hexagonal pieced quilt (p. 18)

Sonia and Hans Scherr-Thoss for photograph of Kharraqan tomb towers, reproduced in their book entitled *Design and Color in Islamic Architecture* (Smithsonian Institution Press, 1968) (p. 19)

Oktay Aslanapa for photograph of Muradiye mosque ceiling, reproduced in his book entitled *Turkish Art and Architecture* (New York: Praeger, 1971) (p. 27)

Topkapi Saray Museum, Istanbul, for "Taking Away of Jam-i-Jihannūma," reproduced in *Turkish Art and Architecture* by Oktay Aslanapa (p. 29)

National Gallery, London, for "The Ambassadors" by Hans Holbein (p. 30)

Archives Photographiques, Paris, for "The Lady and the Unicorn" tapestry, from the collection of the Cluny Museum, Paris (p. 31)

Fogg Art Museum, Harvard University, for the Persian miniature, "Life in the City," c. 1540, reproduced in *The World of Islam* by Ernest Grube (London: Paul Hamlyn Ltd., 1966) (p. 139)

The British Museum, London, for the Froissart tapestry, from the manuscript Froissart's *Chroniques de France et D'Angleterre,* and reproduced in *The Flowering of the Middle Ages,* J. Evans, editor (New York: McGraw-Hill, 1966; London: Thames and Hudson, 1966) (Color Plate 1)

Contents

Playing-card hanging adapted from late fifteenth-century French cards reproduced in *Les Cartes à Jouer* by Henry d'Allemagne.

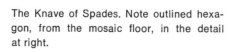

The Knave of Spades. Note outlined hexagon, from the mosaic floor, in the detail at right.

I expect great problems to confound and overwhelm. And they rarely disappoint. Smaller problems on the other hand, being more amenable to solution, are sound antidotes to poisonous feelings of futility. Like crossword puzzles and detective novels they give us the soothing illusion that logic and concentration are certain to yield results. For this reason, I find it dispiriting when a minor perplexity betrays my trust and remains fixed beyond my grasp despite my best efforts to take it in hand and deal with it.

These were my thoughts one late winter afternoon in 1974 as I tried to trace antique Turkish carpet patterns in fifteenth-century Persian miniature paintings. My eyes wandered instead and unbidden to the hexagons clambering like so many *enfants terribles* over the palace walls and floors. They were playing there. Upsetting me. I had long wanted to corral them (and other patterns in the same geometric network) to the squares of the needlepoint canvas. But the hexagon, with the six triangles that compose it, is based on the 60-degree angle, the threads of the canvas on the 90-degree angle and, no matter how I called the tune, I could not get them to dance together.

On the table, to the left of the books I was studying, stood my collection of kaleidoscopes: somber, immobile, hypocritical tubes, their sedate casings hiding the unceasing prismatic gavottes that enliven their hexagonal mirrored chambers. From above, on the wall behind the table, the serene, pure shape of the dignified Shaker cheese basket daunted, its splints forming countless hexagons and six-pointed stars, its base a large hexagon, and its shadow on the wall, with the contrivance of the light, compounding the geometric effrontery.

And it was snowing. Outside my window a corps of white hexagon crystals flocked the pewter dusk. Some might call their choreography beautiful. I called it a conspiracy and retreated to another room to find distraction in putting up my recently completed playing-card hanging (shown unfinished in my last book, *A Pageant of Pattern for Needlepoint Canvas*). The hanging was large, heavy, unwieldy. Had it not been for those disheartening hexagons, I would have waited for assistance. I worked hard, hammered my thumb vigorously, and sat down on the ladder

I looked outside again, sourly. Pewter dusk indeed. Pollution gray with speckles. Behind me, the crookedly hung playing cards were weaving unsteadily on a few tentative nails that were about to desert their burden. As I turned to lend support, my eyes focused on the medieval triangular ground I had selected for Pontus, the Knave of Spades. I had been puzzled by its magnetism, and suddenly, up on the ladder, I understood why it had held me in thrall. Those triangles were making hexagons. And if they could make one hexagonal pattern, surely they might make others.

I finished hanging the cards without further injury to them or to me, descended, picked up needle, yarn, and canvas, and got to work. A small victory and just in time to help me through the enormities of the Six O'Clock News.

Shaker cheese basket, author's collection.

The "play of pattern," when used by professional designers, means the refractory breaking up of solid space so as to produce figures on a surface, usually in a rhythmic, formalized arrangement. The equilateral triangle and its family (hexagons, diamonds, stars, and so forth) give the "play of pattern" a second meaning. Designs based on these geometric forms really do play; they are sportive. Their witty turns and wily puzzles extend to us an invitation to participate in their games; they urge us to discoveries and decisions, and to partner them in reinventing their mercurial surfaces. There is laughter in these patterns and, although most of them were created by sophisticated, superbly inventive, and extraordinarily skilled artists and artisans, they beckon to children as well as adults.

Standing by itself, the equilateral triangle looks a proper, stolid, upright figure. Surround it with neighbors of identical size and shape, start coloring, and watch the flummery start. Designs hop in and out of perspective; two-dimensional surfaces mysteriously deepen into three; modest backgrounds unexpectedly assert themselves and become foregrounds; strutting foregrounds are bested, retire into backgrounds, only to rise again like victorious suns; cubes abound and their concave bodies convex before our eyes; patterns whirl clockwise and reverse direction as though hit by a sudden wind; stars twinkle twice and disappear, dissolving into space; triangles turn cartwheels; ribbons meander like snakes; staid rhombuses become jumping jacks; hexagons take flight like helium balloons; lightning flickers; colors iridesce. Quick-change artists, all of them. It is difficult to observe them as passive spectators; their ambiguities push us toward surmise, their kaleidoscopic riddles toward investigation. Is a spell being cast? If it is, who is doing the casting, they or we?

These "kaleidoscopes" need no manual manipulation, no turning contrivance, to set them dancing. A signal between our eyes and their geometric vitality is all that is required. It should be noted that the designs in this book are entirely dependent on and limited to a single, unchanging geometric form: the equilateral triangle. This strict limitation does not bring us into straitened circumstances. Rather, it reveals how much variety and adventure are to be found within the strictest confinement.

It may be that my description of the animation that enlivens these designs will lead some readers to fear a visual babel, or to wonder whether such initially striking patterns may not, as often happens, become tiresome. But this does not occur. The hexagonal designs, vibrant and shimmering with life, are ordered by a visually nourishing scheme; they have the serenity of a well-planned universe within which the components move gracefully in a coherent plan. They do not pall. They are canny, like magicians who withhold a final trick: a change of light, of viewing angle, of distance will bring surprise.

Early Persian and Turkish miniature paintings show an astonishing number of these patterns, in diverse scales and colors, within a very compressed area. The effect is completely harmonious, even symphonic. The patterns cover every surface that can be made available to them, but they are neither intrusive to the composition nor disconcerting to the eye. There was, I admit, one design, a hyperactive artful dodger, whose gymnastics became unmanageable even while I was stitching it. I gave fair warning: "Don't just do something. Stand there." But it set too fast a visual pace for me, and we parted company.

The optical information to be obtained from a study of the equilateral triangle at work and play is vast, requiring expertise in architecture, eye structure, geometrical theory, and chromatics.

Above: Snow Crystal design, Color Plate 6.

Opposite: Snow crystals. See Color Plate 19 and Hexagonal quilt, page 18.

But I think I have come to understand one of its mysteries: its whirling, twirling, upside-downing, acrobatic mobility. As I noted before, the solitary equilateral triangle looks completely stable; it stands upon one firmly fixed base, with two fixed sides and one fixed apex. But when additional triangles of identical shape and size are placed around it, this stability disappears. Suddenly like a somersault, there are three possible apexes, three possible sides, three possible bases. A peculiar collaboration between the eye and the pattern determines the contours and composition, both of which are subject to reinterpretation—illusions and delusions which a minute will reverse. This transilience in the triangle affects all the larger geometric shapes that grow from it: stars, rhombuses, diamonds, hexagons, and so forth.

When these shapes are colored symmetrically, we generally see the design first this way, then that, and that, and that, in an image progression similar to that of a slide projector. When, as in some modern optical paintings, the color is applied asymmetrically, the metamorphoses are so rapid and mercurial they become visually subversive. See Color Plates 22, 23, 24.

Subversion is a great art, a life-giving catalyst, and it is a pity so few of us have the calling. I mean by this that we are all overheavy with habit. Most of us have known the experience of feeling unexpected appreciation for a broken finger, a damaged leg, even a malfunctioning nose. We look with brand-new thoughts and eyes at old familiars that deserved better from us. Works of genius, though they themselves be wrought from pain, offer this kind of tonic without doing us any injury save that of causing a temporary dislocation while our tired old habits lose their footing. By subverting these, such works present us with new possibilities of thinking, hearing, and seeing—or return to us those we had as children but lost along the way. Many of the examples in the book are what might be called lightweight subverters; they toy with our sense of logic and game with our perceptions.

What of their mysterious insistence on moving into the third dimension, on forming the planes of the cube? The illusion of perspective is closely allied to the relationship between the visual and the tactile. It is said that the infant begins to see depth only after his brain and sense of touch have informed his eye of its existence. Before this, his world—both people and inanimate objects—is perceived as flat surfaces. The visual siphons knowledge from another sense, touch, and then collaborates with the brain on a new three-dimensional outlook. How does the equilateral triangle manage so consistently to force this receding-advancing, concave-convex depth illusion on what the mind and hands know in fact to be flat abstract patterns? It is an enigma, to me anyway; whenever I think I am gaining on an answer, it recedes into the third dimension of my uncooperative brain.

The Color Plates, the Work Pages, and the Sketchbook are meant primarily to serve as guides for projects, but they also carry a considerable amount of historical information, as do some of the notes in other chapters. The Color Plates and the drawings in the Sketchbook document the designs themselves, and the text on the Work Pages and in the Sketchbook gives background material. Much more might be written about the cultures, peoples, and times that produced the designs, but this would be tangential to the main purpose of a project book. There are, however, a few curiosities that might be of some interest to those who, by working them, will become intimates of the designs.

Some scholars believe that the use of hexagonal (triangular

grid) design reflects an advanced society, the presumption being that the square and the circle more easily lend themselvs to duplication, multiplication, and division. Still, many brilliant, sophisticated peoples with strong proclivity for geometric patterning have ignored it. Whether for reasons of unfamiliarity, indifference, or dislike, it is not seen in the works of ancient Greece or Egypt, rarely in those of Assyria. In the Far East the Chinese were not captivated. (The Japanese were more responsive, as evidenced in their baskets, fabrics, woodcuts, wall decorations.) India, otherwise much influenced by Persian design, usually passed it by. The cubic, three-dimensional, mobile, subversive surfaces produced by the 60-degree triangle were given some mild attention by Byzantium, a flirtation that never turned into passion.

It is probably presumptuous to try to isolate a moment of discovery. Man's most glowing achievements may have dim births despite scholarly certainty that they have been brought to light. Achievement does not arise from spontaneous combustion; it is erected on the insights and the failed or fruitful efforts that preceded it. Nevertheless, we humans have an urge to pinpoint. So, and until another finger points elsewhere: hexagonal design, though there are a few examples more variously dispersed in time and place, makes its first flourishing appearance in the densely variegated, almost tumultuously explorative, geometric wall and floor mosaics of first-century Rome. The Roman designers, practical jokers of genius, combined the angles and grids of square, hexagon, pentagon in a fashion that created an extremely strong illusion of depth, undulating motion, and interchanging forms which, with their optical trickery, must have brought moments of panic to those who had to walk upon them. And laughter. For they are very entertaining. A true, if wicked, play ground. Almost every imaginable variety of hexagonal design is encountered here and in the three subsequent centuries. After an extended fallow period, we find them once again, especially the visual acrobats, in the mosaics of twelfth-century Venice, Florence, and Palermo.

But it is in the world of Islam, in the eleventh century, that hexagonal design is truly reborn, sired by the brilliant geometric wizards and noble architects, the Seljuk Turks. (A short detour: I would like to call attention to a group of particularly beguiling panels from late tenth-century Nishapur, now given generous and respectful display room by the Metropolitan Museum of Art, that make original and distinguished use of the hexagon. One of the panels is reproduced in my book, *A Pageant of Pattern for Needlepoint Canvas,* but, to be appreciated, the panels must be seen in reality and in ensemble. They are marvelous.) The Seljuks dominated most of Asia Minor from the eleventh to the fourteenth centuries. Their creative energy is visible in the minarets, medreses, tomb towers, and mosques that still stand in the remains of their strongholds in Turkey and Persia. They re-created and reanimated the Roman repertory, imposing a totally new concept and personality. The Seljuks were not so keenly drawn to the drama and sport of the cubic third dimension and, for the most part, reined the wayward triangle into stable, symphonic rhythms, and more shallow, ribbonlike, interlacement depths. They treated the hexagon as all new toys should be treated, with respect and curiosity; their inventiveness was always wedded to refinement, their playfulness to sobriety and order. Later, under succeeding dynasties, there was occasional loss of restraint, and the Seljuk patterns evolved into the elaborate and labyrinthine arabesques that have neither the dignity nor elegance nor vigor of the originals.

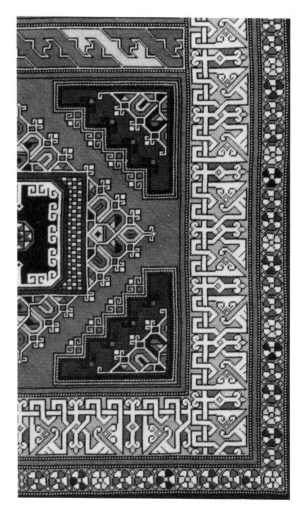

Detail of needlepoint carpet. The secondary border is worked in hexagonal motifs.

The patterns of the Seljuks, modified by color, scale, and a more delicate sensibility, appear in the miniature paintings of Persia and Turkey. There is no missing the obvious relish with which they were painted, and, though the patterns realistically adorn walls, furniture, clothes, and floors, they are also vital and integral elements in abstract composition. Many designs in the book are in debt to these works, and the Work Pages and Sketchbook can be consulted for further acquaintance with their history.

I am perplexed by one particular use of hexagonal design. A number of the early Persian miniature paintings show carpets with geometrically complex field patterns structured on the 60-degree angle. The intricately interlaced hexagonal field designs resemble those in the Turkish carpets (known to us as "Holbeins" because they appear so frequently in his paintings). Surviving fragments of "Holbein" carpets are all based on an octagonal or quartered scheme. The rectilinear organization of the warp and weft of carpet and textile weaving is not unlike that of threads of the needlepoint canvas, which explains why the hexagon/equilateral triangle is so rare in the design repertory of both. The space occupied by the tent stitch in needlepoint can be likened to the space occupied by the knot in the carpet; this small rectangular area is, if not an exact square, usually not very far off. When designing the Turkish carpet (see photographed detail), I selected a secondary border from a curious carpet in a painting by Jan van Eyck, "The Madonna of Canon George van der Poele," Bruges. This border is composed of rows of hexagonal flowers, and, at first glance, it would seem that each of the six petals were identical; each petal in fact has an entirely different outline, contour, and internal shape, and the number of stitches used in the structure of each petal varies greatly. For a really intricate field pattern, a complex reorganization of warp and weft would have been essential, and if such carpets were never actually knotted, it is not likely that the painters would have taken the pains to manufacture them arbitrarily. It is a mystery.

I often wonder as I look at the early carpets whether their designers did not make use of an instrument similar to the kaleidoscope. Although the kaleidoscope seems to be a modern English invention (Sir David Brewster, in 1815), it carries within it the mathematical, optical, colorful, pattern-loving personality of the Middle East, and, in a quartered, hexagonal, or octagonal form, it would have been an evocative tool for textile and tile design.

After this happy birth, the hexagon moved quickly westward, and there are examples of its travels in the chapters that follow. Today quilt collectors are placing similar patterns on contemporary walls, and the effect is startling, so closely does it approximate the tiled and painted surfaces of the Persian palaces and pavilions. It is as if the designs had come full circle, even though their materials and makers are worlds and centuries apart.

We now come to the practical portions of the book. Before going on to the techniques of trianglepoint and to the designs themselves, I would like to pay my respects to an eminent, industrious, and devoted group of pattern designers whose hexagonal patterns are known to all of us, and whose craftsmanship and precision deserve mention. The *Encyclopaedia Britannica* (11th edition) refers to them as "skilled scientists, architects, builders, artisans, laborers." The description fits the Seljuks, but the words were written in praise of the honeybee. Please see the illustration for examples of their expert constructions.

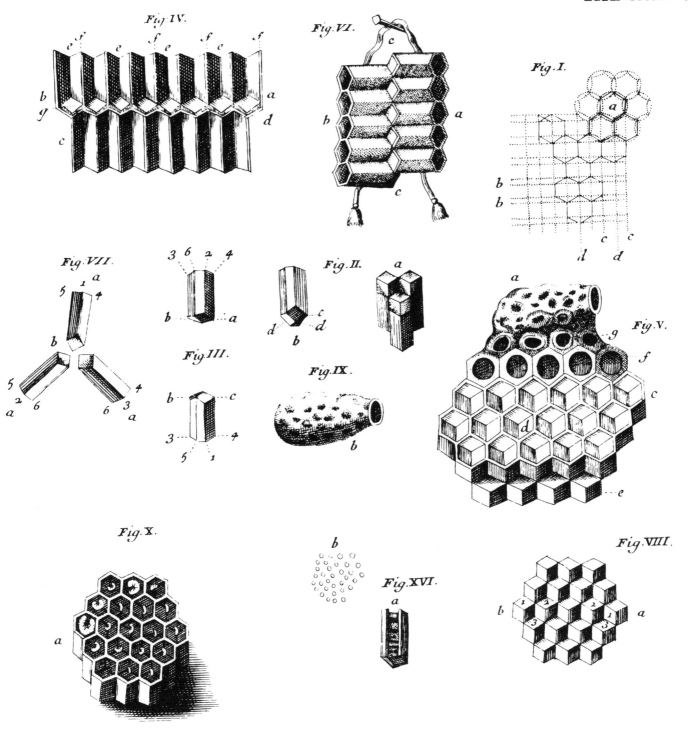

Honeybee hexagonal cellular constructions.
Diagrams from the *Biblia Naturae* by Jan
Swammerdam, 1738.

3 Introduction to Trianglepoint

Trianglepoint has no past. It is a new structural system for applying yarn to needlepoint canvas. This structure makes available to the canvas a vast, hitherto unused, brilliant repertory of hexagonal designs. Many of the designs were devised and executed in sundry media by the magnificently skilled artists and artisans who left for our astonished inspection the shimmering, disciplined abstract surfaces that animate the Persian and Turkish miniature paintings, tiles, enamels, and architectural brickwork of the eleventh through sixteenth centuries; the Islamic and European floor, ceiling, and wall mosaics of the Middle Ages and the Renaissance; the American and English patchwork quilts of the nineteenth and twentieth centuries. Though the right angles made by the squares of the canvas threads were discouragingly inhospitable to the 60-degree angles of the hexagon and equilateral triangle, I had hoped that someday, somehow, an existing technique would, if I kept my eyes open, handily declare itself. I had not thought to originate this technique myself, and, even as I write this, I think I may yet be rescued by a squad of historical precedents. But my extensive research gives me no reason to think it likely. Too bad. I much prefer rediscovering to discovering. Further, I am severely and eccentrically allergic to having to name anything. The truth is, I was uncomfortable having to name my own dog. At times, I gaze at my beloved Blazer, now eight years old, and wonder what her real name is. And my son hasn't divulged his either.

But it became apparent that a name was becoming a matter of urgent convenience. How many times could I write out "this new system of triangular needlework?" or some similar verbal nuisance? My friend Laura Odell suggested "trianglepoint." For this and for her warm and enthusiastic response to these designs and this technique, I thank her. Trianglepoint seems a common-sensible solution, conveying, as it does, the combined idea of the architecture of the stitches (triangle) with the process of needlepoint (yarn, canvas, needle).

While I am still malingering on this subject, I can report that I was no less miserable about having to find names for the designs in the Color Plates and the Sketchbook. Many of them had endured —no, thrived—through centuries without any upstart nomenclature from me. Nonetheless, something had to be done to enable readers and workers to use a practical index to the designs—otherwise they would be forced to treasure-hunt through the pages, all the while harboring dark intentions toward a thoughtless author; it might take more time to find the design than to stitch it. Names again. Lots of them. I have tried to choose words with some causal relationship to the visual, architectural, or historical aspects of the patterns, and I believe that in the main I have successfully ducked the arch, the arbitrary, and the whimsical. Still, I have misgivings and offer apologies to any scholar out there, and to the scold within myself, for any liberties taken—even under the umbrella of function.

It will be noticed that triangle is, more often than not, written in italics. *Triangle* refers to the **structural element** in trianglepoint work. It is most helpfully thought of as a stitch like tent, cross, Florentine, Hungarian point (bargello). The italic type distinguishes it from the triangle that is an **element of design,** and to which I need also to refer. To clarify: This hexagon is composed of six *triangles,* this star is composed of twelve *triangles,* **but** the design will have a pattern of gold triangles and red stars. This looks more complicated than it is; it will be readily understood after a few rows or motifs in one of the designs have been worked.

Detail from Persian miniature, *The Khamsa of Nizami,* "King Khusrau Seated Upon His Throne," sixteenth century. The Metropolitan Museum of Art, New York. See Color Plate 7.

Persian miniature painting, "Iskandar in a Magic Garden," 1435, the Chester Beatty Library, Dublin. See Color Plate 14.

Trianglepoint is surprising because it is so easy to learn, so rapid to work, so uncomplicated and constant in its structure. It requires no complex graphs, charts, or diagrams, no numerical instructions, no counting of minute canvas squares. It makes possible an instant rescaling that can metamorphize the design of a miniature pillow into a wall hanging without the need of perplexing calculations.

The architecture of stitch and design is clean, clear, and readable both in the Color Plates and in the black-and-white photographs in the Work Pages. The stitched examples efficiently act as **their own diagrams**, obviating the need for discouraging technical instructions. This is particularly pleasing to those who never before worked with needle and canvas; they happily embark on ambitious wall hangings within twenty or thirty minutes after being introduced to the basic method. The illustrations in the Trianglepoint Basics chapter give the foundation for a secure journey to the end of work. There should be no unexpected trip-ups on the way, no pit to fall in, nor is any special dexterity needed for practical skills to be quickly developed.

17

Geometric star pieced quilt, 1812. The New-York Historical Society, New York. See Color Plate 34 and the Sketchbook, Drawing 2.

Hexagonal pieced quilt, c. 1880. The American Museum, Bath, England. See Color Plate 19 and snow crystal photograph, page 10.

I am happy, too, that I stumbled on a system so considerate, so economical of time and labor. Like Columbus, I was really looking for something else—but finding a method for getting hexagonal designs onto the squared canvas brought in its cheerful wake this useful additional attraction. The long stitches make for quick work, even on fairly fine canvas. I have a small guest room asking for attention, and I have a budget asking for frugality. Taking my cue from the Persian palaces and pavilions, which employed geometric patterns as though they were precious jewels, I am going to try to make the room gleam with wall hangings, floor cushions, daybed pillows, and a ceiling decoration, using the designs from the Color Plates and the Sketchbook in related, harmonious tones. The large pieces will be stitched on #14 canvas with big *triangles*. All of this would be a grand folly, labor brought to ostentation, if it were to be attempted in the usual needlepoint stitches, such as tent stitch or brick stitch. In the past, speedy needlepoint was most often dependent on the use of very coarse, large-squared canvas that brought a concomitant and noticeable coarseness to the stitch and texture. Trianglepoint does not require this aesthetic sacrifice.

How To Start

I believe that the best beginning is to begin, a technique that has often proved helpful to me when I have embarked on the unfamiliar. My approach, were I new to this book, would be to:

1. Read all the way through, from beginning to end, scanning the pages very lightly. Glance at all illustrative material: Color Plates, black-and-white photos, Sketchbook drawings. In other words, take a skimming, unserious excursion through the book.
2. Select two patterns from the blue-and-white Mosaic Sampler Pillow, Color Plate 2, consult the corresponding Work Pages, and try out a few rows on a discardable piece of canvas. Errors and perplexities will help to clarify, so be very relaxed about it all.
3. Having done this, you will find that your questions and doubts have crystallized. Return to the Trianglepoint Basics chapter for a careful concentrated reading. It will be more intelligible, more useful, more relevant this time around when you come armed with your own questions. Questions that we do not ourselves devise bring answers we cannot absorb. A short rehearsal with a few patterns will provide a frame of reference and a focus.

After you have completed one or two designs, you may have little need to consult the directions that appear on the Work Pages under the heading of Practical. A glance at them, plus a careful inspection of the Color Plate and the black-and-white illustration, will probably suffice. But I urge that you not overlook the really valuable material to be found under Use and Source; much of it can be applied to other designs and to articles of completely different utility.

Brick patterns from the Kharraqan tomb towers, eleventh century, western Iran. Note pattern on right. See Color Plate 30.

4 Trianglepoint Basics

STITCHING THE FIRST TRIANGLE

The Knot and the First Stitches (Figures 2:a–b)

Knot the yarn at one end. The needle enters the canvas from the **upper** side of the canvas, proceeding downward into and through the hole, emerging on the underside of the canvas. This act places the knot on the **upper** side of the canvas. The needle emerges an inch or so to the right of the knot, and one or two canvas rows below the knot, for the first stitch of the *triangle.* After several *triangles* have been worked, their stitches will cover and secure the strand of yarn that runs, on the underside, from the knot to the first stitch. When the strand is completely covered, the knot is scissored off, carefully and very close to the canvas. Do not pull the knot while cutting. Some needle artisans use this initial knot system throughout, for any type of stitch, claiming that it makes a cleaner and less snarled back.

The stitches of all *triangles,* irrespective of size, **always** graduate up and down by **two** canvas threads. The first stitch travels over two canvas threads, the second over four canvas threads, the third over six, and so forth. This never varies. The pieces can be worked with horizontal or vertical stitching (I prefer the latter), as shown in Figure 1. Turn the book so that the Color Plate is in the correct direction. The reverse side of the canvas will show long, slanted stitches. See Figure 2:c.

When the knot is placed to the left of the *triangle* as shown, the *triangle* is worked from **right** to **left.** The knot can be placed to the right of the triangle, which will then be worked from left to right. In either case, make certain that the knot is placed a row or two above the base line, so that the underside stitches catch and secure the strand that extends from the knot to the first stitch.

The stitched *triangle* shown in Figure 2:b is upright (point up). The inverted *triangle* (point down) can be stitched in identical fashion with the upright, the first stitch commencing from the "base" line (the base is now on top) or from the diagonal lines created by the sides of the previous *triangle,* whichever proves most efficient and comfortable.

Each row of trianglepoint has one horizontal line of upright *triangles* and one horizontal interlocking line of inverted *triangles.* When color and design permit, stitch the upright row first, then stitch the inverted row on the return journey. This sequence should always be used for any large areas of solid colors. For the completed first *triangle,* see Figure 2:b. In Figure 2:c the stitches are shown as they appear on the reverse side of the canvas.

Starting Work and Binding Off (Figure 2:d)

Except when working the very first *triangle* on the canvas, where there are no surrounding stitches to provide a hitching post for the yarn, the process of starting new yarn and binding off the old is identical. The needle is run in and out of the previous stitching, on the reverse side of the canvas, journeying about three-quarters of an inch in one direction and about half an inch on the return. The round trip is necessary because trianglepoint is composed of long stitches that may otherwise not provide secure mooring for the ends of yarn. This double action ensures that no raveling takes place during work or the blocking process.

CLOSING THE DIAMOND

When two *triangles* (one upright, point up—one inverted, point down) are placed one above the other in the same color of yarn (Figures 2:e and f), they will make a diamond-shaped rhombus. It

figure 1

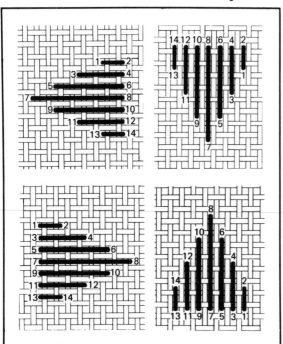

is a good idea, I think, to close the sides of these diamonds—that is, to make one long stitch over the four canvas threads rather than two small stitches over the four canvas threads. The longer stitch interrupts the perforated horizontal lines between the rows of *triangles*. After a little time this closing of the diamond becomes a habit. If at first it is forgotten once or twice, there is no need to rip. The error can be repaired by overstitching (working the long stitch over the two smaller stitches). This will be invisible if done with care and not often. Closing the diamond, while advisable, is not essential. Remember, closing applies only when the two *triangles* that form the diamond are of the same color.

LAYING THE YARN

Trianglepoint requires smooth, easy stitching—a relaxed but disciplined hand. The yarn must be laid across the canvas without stress or slack. The surface must be smooth to form a proper liaison with the mosaic nature of the designs.

The example (Figure 2:g) shows trianglepoint worked with both excessive and inconsistent tension. This produces an unsightly, irregular, overprominent perforation line. The best way to avoid this is as follows:

The **right** hand (sorry, but left-handed workers will have to do their usual vice-versa reading) holds the needle and yarn **underneath** the canvas. This hand pushes the needle through the canvas upward from below where the needle is received by the **left** hand, which awaits it **above** the canvas. The left hand, having received the needle, proceeds to push it downward through the canvas where the needle will, in turn, be received by the right hand. The hands work reciprocally, feeding each other, in a two-step action. Most needlepoint is worked in a one-step, down-and-up action. But in trianglepoint the longer stitches near and including the peak of the *triangle* tend, in a one-step action, to pull the canvas threads together, creating distortion. The two-step method requires that the right hand adjust to working "blind"—to finding the right canvas hole by feeling instead of seeing. An initial awkwardness can quickly be overcome with practice.

BACKSTITCHING

Backstitching, when used, is a final step after the ground has been worked. The backstitch is **always** laid across the diagonal and horizontal perforated lines made by the *triangles* unless otherwise indicated. It journeys from the peak stitch of one *triangle* to the peak stitch of the next nearest *triangle,* diagonally or horizontally, as the case may be. For an example of partially worked backstitching, see Figure 3:a.

Backstitching requires very fine yarn because, in these designs, it is meant to approximate very fine line drawing. It should rest discreetly and slightly subsurface along the sides of the *triangles*. If the yarn is the sort that can be split, a strand or two can be extracted for backstitching. Among the yarns that offer this advantage are the Persian types now being manufactured here and in other countries, French seven-strand silk, and Nantucket worsted. When dividing, place one end of the yarn between the thumb and forefinger of the left hand, holding and gently pulling those strands desired. The right hand **slides** the remaining strands (which will, of course, be saved for future use) down the shaft being held by the left hand; a gliding progression, accordion style, will separate the strands in the right hand from those in the left. Do **not** attempt to peel the yarn off like a banana skin; it will balk, snarl, and break. Fine wools such as crewel (found in all countries supplying

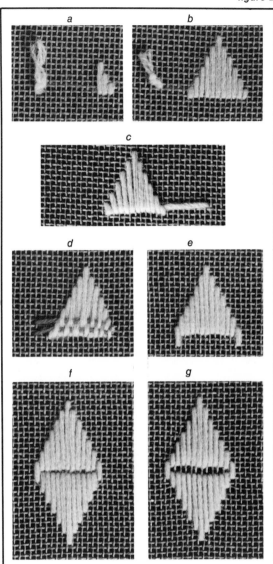

figure 2

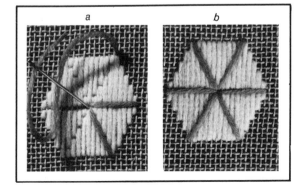

figure 3

needlepoint materials) and the aristocratic Médicis will also serve well. The backstitch in the designs in this book is most often worked in a dark color not found in the design itself, or in white, so matching up dyes is no problem.

All six angles of the hexagon are shown completed in Figure 3:b. I have used too-thick yarn for the sake of visibility. Please consult the Color Plates and the black-and-white photographs for examples of more refined backstitching.

MAKING THE BASIC GEOMETRIC FORMS

These forms are the foundation of the designs in trianglepoint. Their geometric patterns are shaped entirely by the colors used. The application of tone and shade to the *triangles* produces the stars, hexagons, rhombuses. The *triangle* itself is constant in any one design. The *triangles,* being invariable, can be thought of as pre-cut mosaic pieces. The way in which these pieces, all of the same size but diversely colored, are arranged and conjoined makes the hexagons, stars, ribbons, and cubes that form the designs.

The *Triangle* (Figure 4:a)

The Three Rhombuses (Figure 4:b)

Each rhombus is made of two *triangles.* The rhombus on the right, formed by one upright *triangle* sitting atop one inverted *triangle,* is usually called a diamond in the text—to distinguish it from the two slanting rhombuses.

The Hexagon (Figure 4:c)

The hexagon is made of six *triangles.*

The Six-pointed Star (Figure 4:d)

The six-pointed star is made of twelve *triangles.*

THE MOST COMMON DIVISIONS OF THE HEXAGON

Two Triskeles (Figure 4:e)

Three light triangles radiate from a common center (one triskele); three dark triangles radiate from a common center (second triskele).

Two Diamonds and Two Triangles (Figure 4:f)

Each diamond is made of two *triangles.*

The Cube (Figure 4:g)

Each cube is made of three rhombuses; one rhombus forms one side of the cube; each rhombus is made of two *triangles.*

Two Half-Hexagons (Figure 4:h)

Each half-hexagon is made of three *triangles.*

Two Rhombuses and Two Triangles (Figure 4:i)

Each rhombus is made of two *triangles.*

GRAPHED ILLUSTRATIONS

Most of the geometric figures drawn in Figure 5 on isometric graph paper have been illustrated, stitched in trianglepoint, on this page. They are presented again as drawings to supplement the stitched examples and to offer an alternative to those who may find diagrams a helpful medium from which to study the architectural structure of trianglepoint. In addition, I believe that readers who will be venturing into the pages of the Sketchbook or onto uncharted ground of their own will find it advantageous to see how the drawings translate into needleworked hexagons, cubes, diamonds, and rhombuses, and vice versa.

Each triangle on the graph represents one stitched *triangle* on canvas. The size of the stitched *triangle,* as you will see in the following pages, varies with the design; the height and width of the *triangle* depends on the number of stitches used to erect it.

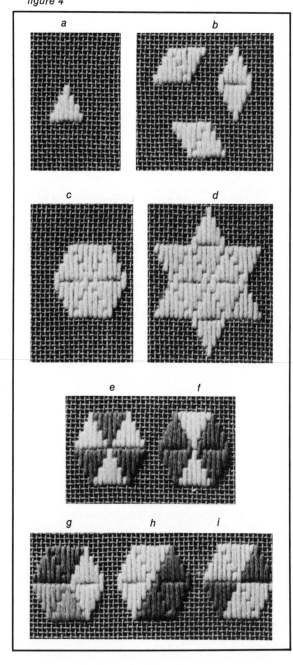

figure 4

a   b

c   d

e   f

g   h   i

Neither the equilateral triangle nor the hexagon has seen any real use on the counted canvas before. The technique of trianglepoint makes this new union functional. I have made a beginning—but there are many possibilities still to be explored, many intriguing designs still to be realized by modern hands. In drafting new designs and variations on graph paper you must use **isometric** graph paper; the common squared graph paper will not do, because it is constructed on the 90-degree angle. Unfortunately, isometric graph paper is not easily obtained in art-supply stores, nor are the staffs in these stores very responsive to inquiries about possible sources, but it may be ordered directly from the printer, The Keuffel and Esser Company, 40 East 43rd Street, New York, N.Y. 10017 (for city residents only; all other inquiries should be addressed to 20 Whippany Road, Morristown, N.J., 07960). The paper measures 7 × 10 inches, with four triangles to the inch; the order number is 46 4231, and the sheets may be ordered singly or in quantity. If there is a school of architecture or design in your city, there will probably be a local supplier. See the pages at back of the book for examples of isometric graphing.

FINISHING

Edging the Hexagon (Figure 6:a)

The edging is made after the hexagonally shaped design has been completed. The edging, here stitched in the darker tone, is worked in the same type of stitch as that used for trianglepoint, but the stitches are uniform instead of graduated in length. When worked thus, the stitch is known as the straight or upright Gobelin. It can span whatever length is best suited to the canvas, traveling over three, four, or five threads. Very fine canvas will require a longer Gobelin stitch; otherwise the edge it gives will be too narrow for seaming or hemming. Coarser canvas will require a shorter Gobelin. The Gobelin edge will be invisible; its function is to provide a sort of selvage for sewing so that the hem or seam will not intrude upon the area of the design.

Please note the twin alignment of the stitches that traverse the **diagonal** edges. These stitches, always the same length, climb the four slanted sides of the hexagon, always two by two. One of the twins uses the canvas hole already occupied by the trianglepoint stitch; the other uses the hole immediately under the trianglepoint stitch. The stitches of the **horizontal** rows use the holes already occupied by trianglepoint stitches. If you prefer, vertical stitches can be worked along the slanted sides. Make them slightly longer than the stitches on the horizontal (top and bottom) sides.

Edging the Rectangle (Figure 6:b)

The edging is made after the entire rectangularly shaped design has been completed. The horizontal rows of Gobelin stitch, as above, use canvas holes already occupied by the trianglepoint stitches. The vertical rows of Gobelin stitch use the holes immediately **under** the final, outer trianglepoint stitch. Note the two unworked squares near the corner. This avoids bulk when seaming.

CANVAS (Selecting Direction and Measuring)

The trianglepoint method, though it comes close, cannot give an absolutely true equilateral triangle; that is, the base line of the stitched triangle will always measure a little shorter than that of the side, making the triangle slightly higher than broad. Our object is to keep this discrepancy minimal. It is necessary to examine the structure of the needlepoint canvas itself to see if we can use its

figure 5

5. Line 1: the equilateral triangle; the three rhombuses (two slanted, one diamond-shaped); the hexagon, the six-pointed star. Line 2: rescaled triangles, rhombuses, hexagon, star. Line 3: larger rescaled triangles, rhombuses, hexagon, star. Line 4: triskele, two diamonds, cube, two half hexagons, two rhombuses, and two triangles. Line 5: two cubes rescaled, tonal values exchanged.

figure 6

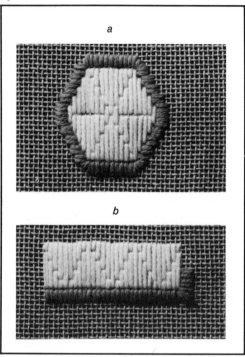

figure 7

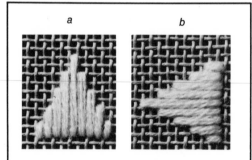

properties to assist us in this aim. Surprisingly, the interwoven threads, contrary to our expectations, are usually not spaced evenly. The horizontal threads may be slightly more compressed than the vertical; conversely, the vertical threads may lie more closely together than the horizontal. This means that the square formed by canvas threads will have sides that are not quite equidistant. This works to our advantage. Whenever possible, the vertical stitches of trianglepoint should travel over those canvas threads that have the shortest distance between them. The fastest way to make a determination is to stitch two test *triangles* (Figures 7:a and 7:b). Measure them from base to tip. Stitch the canvas in the direction that produces the **shortest** *triangle.* The variance between the heights of the two test *triangles* will be barely perceptible, but it multiplies as the work continues. The test must be reapplied each time new canvas is employed because the manufacturing process does not yield consistent results.

There are times when the proportion of the article being made must take precedence over our wish to make the shortest possible *triangle.* In other words, the size of a large wall hanging will have to dictate the manner in which the canvas is directed. But the slight geometric imbalance in the *triangle* need cause no real concern. The antique village and nomadic carpets of Anatolia (Turkey) and Persia (Iran), to me the most beautiful of all Oriental carpets, often show a similar disproportion in the patterns based on the angles of the square; the warp and weft of the loom produce a knot with sides that are not quite equal. This peculiarity, creating medallions, geometric flowers, and animals and stars that are slightly off in measure, brings a noticeable vivacity and visual interest to compositions that might be static if all were serene mathematical perfection.

It is wise to calculate the approximate size of your finished design. When you know this in advance of work, you can cut your canvas accordingly. Even so, always leave generous margins. In the event of miscalculation or unexpected good ideas (borders, for example) you will not be caught short.

The Work Pages give the dimensions of all the pieces in the Color Plates, but it should be remembered that the canvas is not always consistently woven. Some #14 canvases actually measure fifteen or thirteen threads to the inch, and similar discrepancies will be found in the other gauges. Nevertheless, the finished size of your piece should not vary very much from the finished size as shown in the illustration and from the dimensions given on the Work Pages.

But what of variations, original designs, or those based on the drawings in the Sketchbook? What areas will they occupy? After stitching the first *triangle,* measure its width and height. Then go to the design and count the number of *triangles,* both vertically and horizontally (there will not be many in either direction). Multiply the number of *triangles* by their measurements, down and across. You can do this mathematically or by marking the ruler with the height and width of the *triangle,* and ticking off the *triangles* as you slide the ruler along the canvas. This is my method, and it works fast and efficiently. The triangles in any design are so few that the measuring of prospective size offers no problem and you will never have to count small canvas squares. **Always think in terms of triangles**. The square plays no part in trianglepoint except as a foundation for the graduated stitches.

RESCALING THE DESIGNS

Rescaling Method One

The number of stitches used to construct the *triangle* can be increased or decreased, thereby making the *triangle* larger or smaller.

The number of *triangles* forming the design remains unchanged; the alteration in the size of the *triangle* itself causes the scale of the entire design to alter in kind.

The Largest *Triangle* (Figure 8:a)

There are thirteen stitches in this *triangle*. The peak stitch travels over fourteen canvas threads.

The Second Largest *Triangle* (Figure 8:b)

There are eleven stitches in this *triangle*. The peak stitch travels over twelve canvas threads.

The Third Largest *Triangle* (Figure 8:c)

There are nine stitches in this *triangle*. The peak stitch travels over ten canvas threads.

The Smallest *Triangle* (Figure 8:d)

There are seven stitches in this *triangle*. The peak stitch travels over eight canvas threads.

These four *triangles* are used throughout the book, 8:b and 8:c more frequently than 8:a and 8:d. The perfect all-around partner for trianglepoint is #16 needlepoint canvas. It works well in conjunction with all these *triangles,* with almost all yarns. It yields a smooth, refined surface. Its threads, neither too fine nor too coarse, allow work to be accomplished with extreme rapidity, and serves both small and large articles. Do not try to make a *triangle* with fewer stitches than 8:d; the triangular contour will be lost. A larger *triangle* than 8:a may make the stitches too long and unwieldy. Make certain that the yarn covers the canvas adequately—there may have to be adjustments for the various *triangle* sizes; some use longer stitches than others. Adjust the yarn if it is too thick or thin. The aim is a smooth, flatly covered surface.

Rescaling Method Two

Method Two **multiplies** the *triangles* to enlarge scale. This method is used exclusively for **increasing** size. If, however, a design has been conceived by Method Two, the scale may be made smaller by reversing the process.

A large triangle made of nine *triangles*. (Figure 8:e)

A large triangle made of four *triangles*. (Figure 8:f)

The *triangle* used to construct 8:e and 8:f. (Figure 8:g)

A large triangle made of four *triangles*. (Figure 8:h)

The *triangle* used to construct 8:h. (Figure 8:i)

Obviously, when working on a design, this method is applied in equal multiples to the other geometric forms. In other words, if the number of *triangles* that form a large triangle is tripled, the number of *triangles* used to construct the rhombus or cube will be similarly tripled. See Color Plate 24.

Rescaling Method Three

Method Three is, of course, not confined to trianglepoint; it is applicable to just about all forms of needlepoint. With this method, the **ground** on which the *triangle* will be worked is altered by the selection of a larger- or smaller-gauge canvas (see Figures 9:a–e). Gauge is the count of canvas threads to the inch. Gauge #16 means that there are sixteen threads to the inch, #14, fourteen threads to the inch. The more threads to the inch, the finer the canvas; therefore, the higher the gauge number, the finer the canvas.

All three rescaling methods can be combined: (Method One) Changing the number of stitches within the *triangle*. (Method Two) Multiplying the *triangles*. (Method Three) Changing the size of the *triangle* by changing the canvas gauge.

When employing Method Three, particular attention must be given to ensure that the yarn is suited in weight and thickness to the canvas. If it is too thin, it will not cover and the threads of canvas

figure 8

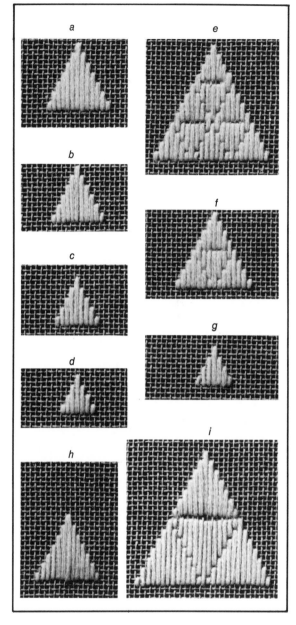

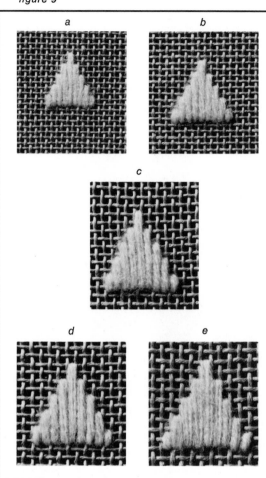

figure 9

a

b

c

d

e

will obtrude. If it is too thick, the surface will look too woolly and bulky. Ecru canvas is the least likely to permit its threads to make an unwelcome appearance, but white canvas is also fine, provided the yarn is not too thin—especially when it is in a very dark tone, such as navy or black. A large monotone background area can be painted with oils, acrylics, or indelible marker, before stitching, in the color of the dark yarn. Or, in the rare, critical situation, a prudent touch-up can be applied, after stitching, with indelible marker, with, as *The I Ching* says, "No Blame."

The canvas is shown in actual size. Mono is the colloquial name for canvas that is woven in single-thread structure. Another type of canvas, Penelope, is woven in doubled strands, but it has not been used for the trianglepoint designs.

ARTICLES OF USE

These three methods of rescaling, singly or in combination, are not complicated; they can be learned and put into operation quickly and easily. Because of this, trianglepoint designs are satisfyingly versatile, and they can be used, design intact, for an unusually wide range of articles of very diverse sizes and functions:

SMALL SCALE: Eyeglass cases for pocket or purse or for hanging on the wall near bed pillow or reading chair; slippers; bags; playing-card (and other) box tops; tennis-racket covers; diary, address (and other) book covers; trays (under lucite or glass); covers for hot-water bottles (now making a necessary comeback); frames for mirrors; straps for luggage stands; valances; small pillows.

MEDIUM SCALE: Pillows; floor cushions; back throws for club chairs and sofas; dining-chair upholstered seats; floor "chairs" (one cushion for the floor—one cushion, in identical size, for the backrest against the wall, worked in the same colors and pattern, or in a different pattern in the same or related colors); fireplace screens (the mosaic designs are ideal for vertical panels); wall hangings.

LARGE SCALE: Larger floor cushions and wall hangings; table carpets; ceiling decorations; paneled screens. I think that a design like Transilient Prisms Wall Hanging, Color Plate 23, would adapt superbly to such use. A three-panel screen might be worked with cubes of different colors for each panel. The length of the stitches will make the work go very quickly; altering the colors will make the process of work entertaining.

In addition to the ease with which they can be transformed from tiny to grand scale, the designs have the advantage of visual adaptability. Structural and chromatic relationships often suffer great damage when subjected to dramatic reproportioning, and many designs look eccentric or mutilated when such adaptations are imposed. The designs in the book—protected by their hexagonal geometric structure and some curious, even inexplicable, compositional mystery—are gratifyingly pliable in this respect. The small, twinkling patterns that enrich the tiny floors and walls of the palaces and pavilions in Persian miniature paintings look as clear, as interesting, and as effective as they do in their full-size, real-life versions, and vice versa; this applies as well to the conversion of triangle-point examples—from large wool wall hanging to tiny silk pillow (see photographs of the Muradiye ceiling design, opposite, and the Turkish miniature "Taking Away of Jam-i-Jihannūma," page 29).

When the subject of rescaling arises, I often allude to table carpets and ceiling decorations—terms that ask for clarification:

Ceiling decoration in the Muradiye mosque,
1426, Bursa, Turkey, the first Ottoman
capital. See Color Plates 25 and 26.

Table Carpets

The hand-knotted Turkish carpet of the Late Middle Ages and Early Renaissance is one of the joys of European religious painting. The painters, contemporaries of the Turkish carpet artists, depicted the designs with utmost fidelity—an exactitude that can have been based only on the greatest respect, passion, and affection. Even now, the loving, fastidious testimony of the hands of Holbein, Van Eyck, Memling, Lotto, Crivelli, and many more allows us to see not only long-vanished patterns but also the use to which the carpets were put by the Western personages who housed them.

That they were affluent personages there can be no doubt. Carpets were listed in inventories and wills along with sculpture and paintings—and they were just as costly. There was competition among the powerful figures of Church and State to acquire these textiles of glorious color and craft. The Church, despite her fierce hatred and contempt for the so-called Saracen or Moor, was an avid collector. Not only did her abhorrence not extend to the work of the "Saracen's" hand, filled though this work might be with the profound and unmistakable emblems of Islamic religion, culture, and artistry, but a most intimate and extraordinary relationship developed between these enemies. It is strange to see how often the Turkish carpet warmed and graced the cathedral table, how often it gentled the ground beneath the Madonna's slippers and throne.

If it were not for these great inspirational paintings, the world would know little of the early carpet, and scholars would have difficulty documenting the few that have survived the centuries. Undoubtedly, these paintings helped popularize the carpet, and, shortly thereafter, we see it on the massive library and conference tables of doges, cardinals, kings, and merchant lords. In Venice, the carpets, thus used, were called *tapedi da desco* and *tapedi di tavola.* In the seventeenth century the Oriental carpet, still signifying wealth, power, position, and worldliness, found its way onto the tables of the burghers of Holland and Flanders. Once again the most accomplished painters fell under its spell, and the carpet's portrait was now being painted by the great Vermeer and his contemporaries.

Motivation for ownership aside, the table carpet has dignity, strength, warmth, and visual excitement. And the area of the table is refreshing and unexpected to the modern eye. The kaleidoscopic designs adapted here for trianglepoint are closely related to those of the early carpets, and the rapidity with which they can be worked makes the labor pleasant and the project practical. Antique carpets were often small. The paintings often show them with a short overhang—and this is how, to my eye, they look most handsome. However, if you have the hours and are so inclined, floor length is luxurious and beautiful.

There is no question that most of these designs would look marvelous on the floor. But as a partisan of utility and appropriateness, I cannot advocate their use as carpets or mats (floor cushions, of course, are fine). The long stitches of the *triangle* cannot compete with tent stitch for hardiness and durability, and I would not ask it of them. Yet there are needleworkers who have used Florentine stitching, bargello, and similarly structured stitches for carpets. I don't approve, but if you have done so and don't rue it, then medium-scale trianglepoint offers similar hazards and superior patterns for the floor.

Ceiling Decoration

Textile and tapestry designs were often placed on the ceilings of medieval palaces and chateaux. See Color Plate 1. They were

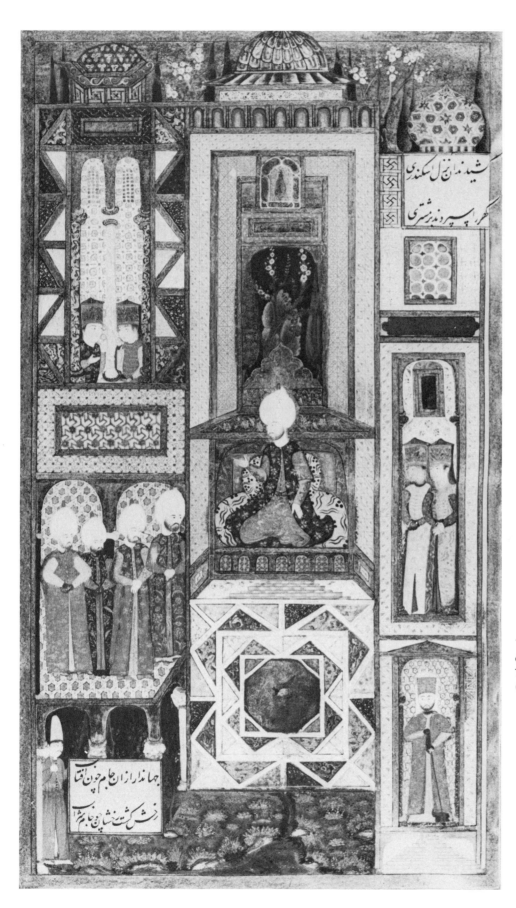

Turkish miniature painting, "Taking Away of Jam-i-Jihannūma," sixteenth century. Topkapi Saray Museum, Istanbul. See Color Plate 15.

Detail from "The Ambassadors," Hans Holbein, 1533. The National Gallery, London. A famous Turkish table carpet.

framed and hung overhead like canopies. Many of the designs in the books are suited to such use. They can be either conventionally framed or wrapped around frames (see the Work Page for Color Plate 24) and then suspended from invisible fishing line. I have emphasized ceiling decoration because so many of the designs are directly derived from mosaics and tiles which themselves ornamented walls and ceilings. The optical fascination of the patterns would suggest their being hung over bed or crib for contemplation and amusement. The ceiling above a dining table provides an area, both limited and clearly defined, that would be enhanced by this treatment.

BLOCKING

The stitches of trianglepoint bring minimal distortion to the canvas. Nevertheless, blocking is important for smoothing and straightening, for correcting alignment and angles, and for general effect. Measure the worked area, being careful not to stretch it, from top to bottom and from side to side. (If the piece is hexagonal, be sure the measure spans the widest and longest areas.) Draw a rectangle on a clean piece of wood in those dimensions. Tack the dry piece, right side down, and adjust the corners and outlines to accord with those drawn on the board. When the piece is hexagonal, make sure the six joints touch the drawn lines. Wet a Turkish towel thoroughly, wring it well, place it upon the canvas. Press the towel with a hot iron. Remove the towel. Steam the canvas by gliding the iron over it without touching. Let it dry. Untack after two hours or so (depending on humidity). The right side can now be lightly pressed under a damp Turkish towel.

You can also block by just steaming and pulling without tacking, although this method is not quite so accurate. And, of course, you can block in the conventional way by wetting your work thoroughly (roll it in soaking Turkish towels) and then tacking as above. At least two or three drying days will be necessary. Whatever method is used, be certain not to stretch the canvas, particularly in the direction of the stitches; if the canvas is stretched, the *triangle* rows will pull away from each other and the perforated lines between the rows will be too obvious.

HANGING

Wall hangings can be border-stitched, as shown in the photograph on page 24, with simple Gobelin stitch, which will be hemmed back. Sew a Velcro strip along the top of the reverse side of the hanging onto the Gobelin hem, which should be made wide enough for this purpose. Then paste a reciprocal Velcro strip onto the wall; press together for adherence. Another method for hanging is this: using the same colors of the borders, or one color only, stitch an additional row or two on all sides, extended like four flaps, leaving the corners between the flaps unworked for mitering. Have a cheap frame constructed to the dimensions of the design (without the extra rows), or a quarter of an inch larger to allow for the stretchability of canvas. Wrap the wall hanging around the frame, stapling to the underside and mitering the corners. This is an appropriate treatment for precise geometric hangings. The alien material and the stiffness of a conventional frame is avoided, and so is the rippling that comes from imprecise blocking, lining, or hanging when no frame is used. Always avoid stifling your warm wool under cold glass; a textile should be warm and supple (trays, table tops, and other surfaces that may suffer severe insult from daily use excepted).

Detail from the tapestry series known as "The Lady and the Unicorn," probably late fifteenth century. The Cluny Museum, Paris. Another celebrated table carpet which, in my judgment, is certainly Islamic in design. The original was probably made in Turkey.

5 Color Plates

Note: The Color Plates are arranged to be used in conjunction with the Work Pages. See page 65.

LIST OF PLATES

1. "Author Presenting His Manuscript to the Comte de Foix," fifteenth-century miniature from the manuscript *Froissart's Chroniques de France et d'Angleterre.*
2. Mosaic Sampler Pillow
3. Cloud Pillow
4. Persian Basket
5. Red Cubes
6. Snow Crystal Kaleidoscope
7. Persian Throne
8. Reflections in Bronze and Steel
9. Shimmering Diamonds
10. Shadow Boxes
11. Mosaic Miters
12. Wreath Kaleidoscope
13. Egyptian Hexapod
14. Blue Persian Tile
15. Persian Carpet Knots
16. Lights and Shadows Kaleidoscope
17. Adriatic Waves
18. Froissart Wall Hanging
19. Snow Flowers
20. Palermo Meander
21. Turkish Tent
22. Harlequin Cube
23. Transilient Prisms Wall Hanging
24. Crystal Wall Hanging
25. Turkish Sky
26. Pieced Quilt Turkish Sky
27. Solar Kaleidoscope
28. Stained Glass Kaleidoscope
29. Snowcaps
30. Seljuk Brick
31. Whirling Hexagons
32. Starred Honeycomb
33. Busby Berkeley's Stars
34. Sunburst Kaleidoscope
35. Stars Within Stars
36. Camera Obscura
37. Grandmother's Flower Garden
38. Seljuk Pinwheels
39. Ribboned Stars
40. Venetian Triangles
41. Refractions
42. Spiral Flowers
43. San Marco Lightning
44. San Marco Stepped Boxes

"Author Presenting His Manuscript to the Comte de Foix," fifteenth century. French miniature from the manuscript "Froissart's Chroniques de France et d'Angleterre." British Library Board, London.

1

See Color Plate 18.

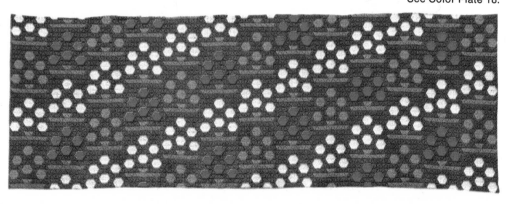

Mosaic Sampler Pillow   **2**
(Work Page 66)

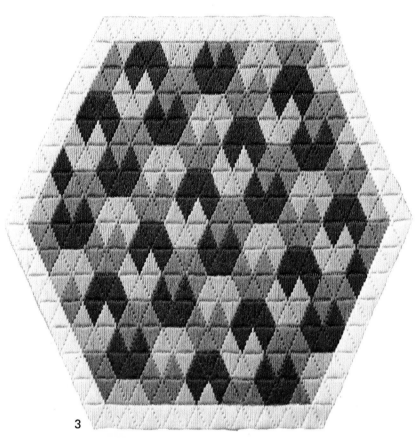

3

Cloud Pillow
(Work Page 70)

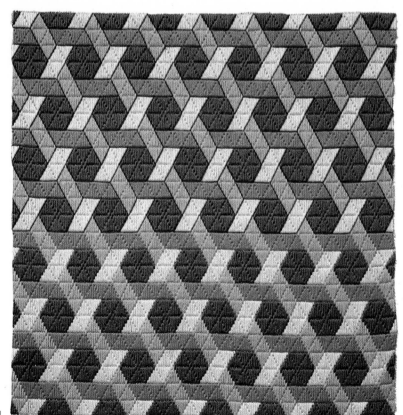

Persian Basket
(Work Page 71)

4

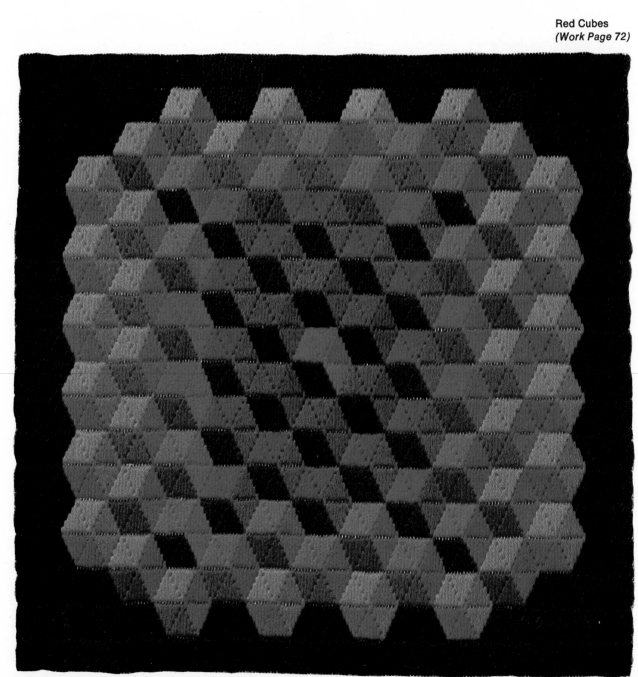

6

Snow Crystal Kaleidoscope
(Work Page 73)

Persian Throne
(Work Page 74)

8

Reflections in Bronze and Steel
(Work Page 75)

9

Shimmering Diamonds
(Work Page 76)

Shadow Boxes
(Work Page 77)

10

Mosaic Miters
(Work Page 78)

11

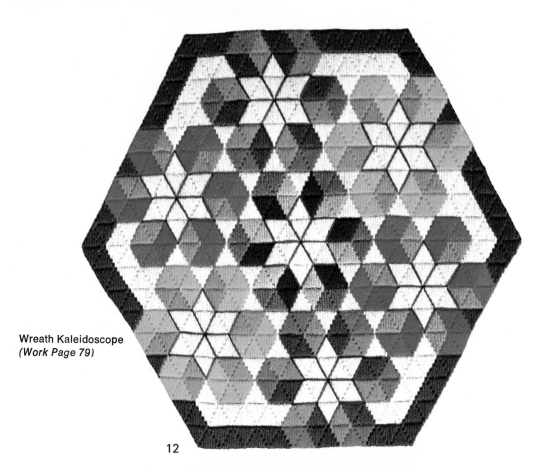

Wreath Kaleidoscope
(Work Page 79)

12

13

Egyptian Hexapod
(Work Page 80)

14

Blue Persian Tile
(Work Page 81)

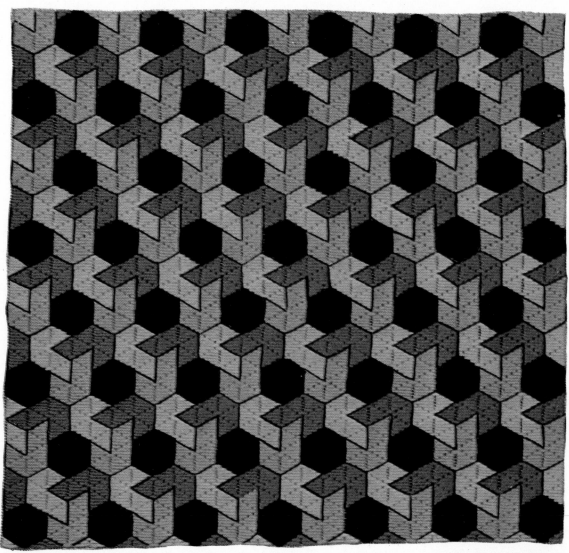

Persian Carpet Knots   **15**
(Work Page 82)

Lights and Shadows Kaleidoscope
(Work Page 83)

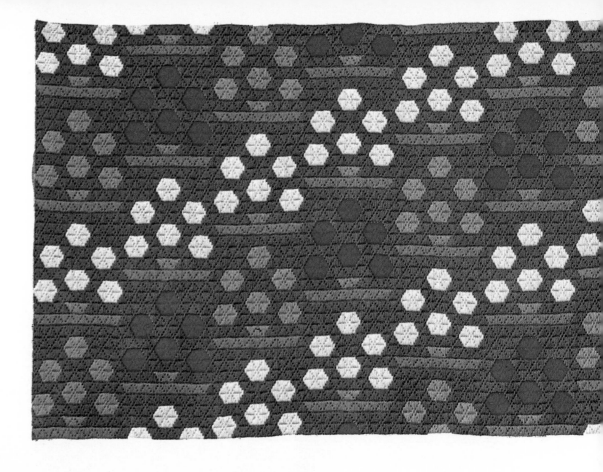

Adriatic Waves
(Work Page 84)

17

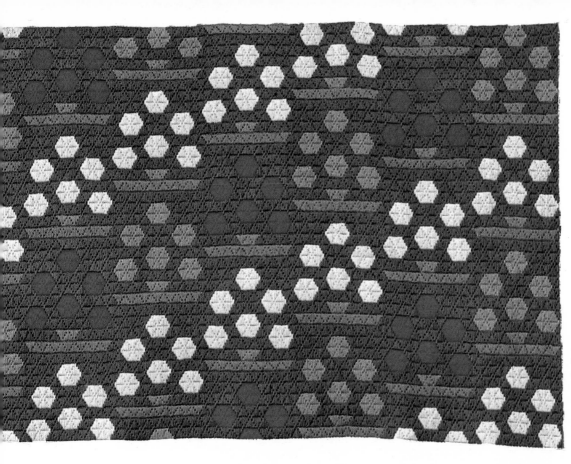

Froissart Wall Hanging
(Work Page 85)
18

Snow Flowers
(Work Page 86)

19

20

Palermo Meander
(Work Page 87)

21

Turkish Tent
(Work Page 88)

Harlequin Cube
(Work Page 89)

Transilient Prisms Wall Hanging
(Work Page 90)

Crystal Wall Hanging **24**
(Work Page 91)

Turkish Sky
(Work Page 92)

25

Pieced Quilt Turkish Sky
(Work Page 93)

26

Solar Kaleidoscope
(Work Page 94)

Stained Glass Kaleidoscope
(Work Page 95)

Snowcaps
(Work Page 96)

29

Seljuk Brick
(Work Page 97)

30

Whirling Hexagons
(Work Page 98)

31

Starred Honeycomb
(Work Page 99)

32

Busby Berkeley's Stars   **33**
(Work Page 100)

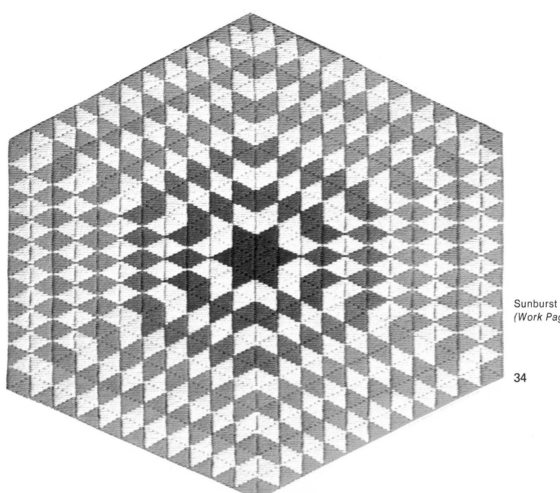

Sunburst Kaleidoscope
(Work Page 101)

34

Stars Within Stars
(Work Page 102)

35

Camera Obscura
(Work Page 103)

36

Grandmother's Flower Garden
(Work Page 104)

37

Seljuk Pinwheels
(Work Page 105)

38

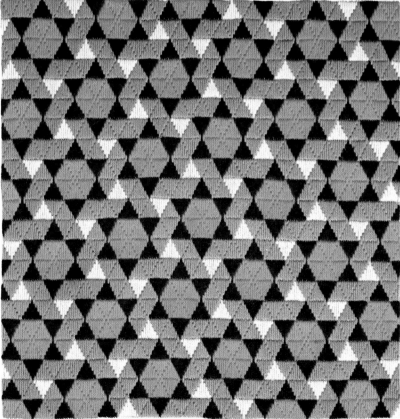

Ribboned Stars
(Work Page 106)

39

Venetian Triangles
(Work Page 107)

40

Spiral Flowers
(Work Page 110)

42

Refractions
(Work Page 108)

41

San Marco Lightning
(Work Page 111)

43

San Marco Stepped Boxes
(Work Page 112)

44

The Work Pages that follow are arranged to be used in conjunction with the Color Plates, which show both title and number for easy cross reference. Because the Plates reproduce the designs in color, they must be consulted for the architecture of the over-all composition, for the sequence of repeat patterns, for the tones, for the general impression that the final design will give. The Work Pages should be consulted for all other practical matters. On each Work Page, you will find the canvas gauge, the number of colors, and the dimensions of the finished design, as shown. (All the designs, with the exception of Color Plate 41, are large enough at least for pillows, and most can be rescaled for ceiling decorations, table carpets, wall hangings, and floor cushions.) Each Work Page will have the *triangle* symbol, which shows at a glance how many stitches were used for the *triangle* in the design. Suggestions for techniques, rescaling, variations in pattern, color, usage, and historical information about the origin of the design will be found in the text.

Cushions and pillows were photographed before they were stuffed, in order to avoid distorting curves and shadows. **The Color Plates act as their own diagrams** (with a little help from the Work Pages), and in this role are best seen flat. If you can afford it, use pure goose down for the filling or goose down coupled with goose feathers.

All the designs in this book use one stitch only: trianglepoint. The *triangle* construction never varies in size or position in any one piece, and once you determine how many stitches you will use to erect your *triangle,* your construction course is set. A few photographs show the *triangle* on its side rather than upright (it is either one or the other in any single design). It may be simpler for some workers to turn the picture halfway around and work the design as an upright *triangle* instead of sideways. The colors of the yarns selected for the *triangles* are what make the design.

The suggested stitching routes are meant to help the worker avoid the laborious, time-consuming task of counting tiny canvas squares. For this reason, the routes always place the basic *triangles* in close proximity, so that the previously stitched *triangle* acts as the lodestar or point of departure for the next stitch. If you find yourself involved in extensive counting of canvas squares, you can assume that there has been some failure of communication, and you may wish to consult the itinerary again. The routes are also meant to establish the easiest path for work. Once you have stitched the first row, you can fill in the surrounding areas with ease. Finished measurement refers to the photographed piece, length preceding width. Trianglepoint is uncomplicated. After your first pattern has been completed, you will probably refer almost exclusively to the Color Plates and black-and-white photographs for guidance.

I believe in plunging fast and only partially prepared into work before asking too many questions; in other words, one should base one's inquiries on personal experience and on real rather than anticipated predicaments, which should be minimal in the case of trianglepoint. If you try out one or two patterns in the Mosaic Sampler Pillow that follows, you will have the ease and pleasure of clear sailing later. The patterns in this pillow design serve as an introduction to all the geometric shapes used throughout the book: triangles, hexagons, stars, rhombuses, diamonds, cubes, half-hexagons. Familiarity with their forms and structures will enable you to undertake with comfort and security all subsequent work. If you want to create variations, sketch your ideas on isometric graph paper, as in the Sketchbook chapter, which begins on page 114.

6 Work Pages

Practical

I selected subdued, earthenware blues because of the number of patterns in the pillow, but other tones or colors, bright or contrasting, can replace these. "Square" is a convenience. Sides are not equal.

SQUARE A Starting at top left, stitch the first blue half-star, then stitch the completed blue star to the right. Finish all blue stars. Fill in white hexagons.

SQUARE B Starting at top left, stitch the first horizontal row of white half-hexagons, then stitch the light blue half-hexagons in the row below, then the white half-hexagons. The dark blue interiors are worked last.

SQUARE C Starting at top left, stitch the dark blue diamonds in a vertical row. Return to the top, stitch the white and medium blue rhombus forms that complete the cubes, also in a vertical row. Continue in the same way.
Note: LEAVE ONE **VERTICAL** CANVAS ROW UNWORKED BETWEEN ALL THE PATTERNS. Remember this when arriving at Squares D, G, and J.

SQUARE D Starting at top left, stitch the very dark blue conic form (incomplete), then stitch the very dark blue complete conic form immediately below, then the next (incomplete). Return to the top, thread a needle with medium blue yarn, another needle with light blue yarn, and a third needle with white yarn, stitch in the zigzag vertical form to the right. Continue until the honeycomb pattern is complete.

SQUARE E Starting at top left, stitch the medium blue corner. Working with two needles, one threaded with the dark blue and the other with the white yarn, stitch the outside, largest hexagonal frame. Work inward, stitching frame by frame, until the center is reached.

SQUARE F Starting at top left, work the first dark blue triangle, then work the white triangle to the immediate right. Complete the vertical row of white diamonds under the white triangle. Stitch the "cables" to the right of the white diamond row, working with three needles, each threaded with one of the three tones of blue.

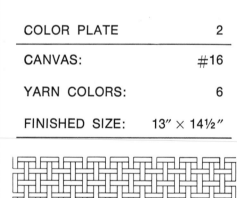

COLOR PLATE	2
CANVAS:	#16
YARN COLORS:	6
FINISHED SIZE:	13″ × 14½″

67

SQUARE G Leave one vertical row of canvas holes unworked. Starting at top left, stitch the first blue triangle, then the second below and to the right. Continue the diagonal row. Then stitch the diagonal row of white triangles, and so forth.

SQUARE H Starting at top right, stitch one diagonal row of the dark blue half-hexagons, descending leftward. This establishes the route for the other half-hexagons.

SQUARE I Starting at top right or left, stitch the first horizontal row of long rhombus forms, working with two needles, each threaded in one of the two tones of blue. Then work the second horizontal row of short rhombuses with two needles, one threaded with blue, one threaded with white yarn, and complete the rest.

SQUARE J Leave one vertical row of canvas holes unworked. Start at top left, stitch the first dark blue diamond, then the lighter blue diamond below and on its right. Continue to work all the blue diamonds in this sequence. Then fill in the small white diamonds.

SQUARE K Starting at top left, stitch the first navy blue hexagon, then all the hexagons below in the vertical row. Return to the top and stitch the next vertical row of hexagons.

SQUARE L Starting at top right or left, stitch the first horizontal row of white inverted triangles, then, with two needles, fill in the upright triangles of the first row. Stitch the dark blue triangles of the second row, and so forth.

The last step is to outline the mosaic squares with very fine, dark blue yarn. Work the horizontal lines first, always stitching from the peak of one triangle to the next, using the perforations made by previous stitching. Keep the same canvas thread count for the vertical rows; these are not occupied by previous stitches, but the horizontal rows are.

You can divide the pillow into hexagons rather than squares or other rectangles. If you so decide, you will not have to leave the unworked holes for the final backstitching. The shape of the pillow itself will then be hexagonal.

Use

Pillow. Rescale for wall hanging or floor cushion by increasing the number of stitches within the *triangle*. You can also increase the size of each square by extending the pattern. Each mosaic square is sufficiently interesting to serve as a pattern for an individual floor cushion, or pillow. You can make a series of separate pillows or cushions from the various patterns, using one pattern for each. If you would like to have a really large wall hanging, use #14 canvas **and** increase the number of stitches in the *triangle*.

Source

Every one of the squares derives from artisan work executed in the near or distant past: thirteenth-century Seljuk architectural brick and tiles, fifteenth- and sixteenth-century Persian and Turkish miniature paintings, early and late medieval mosaics in France and Italy, nineteenth- and twentieth-century pieced English and American patchwork quilts.

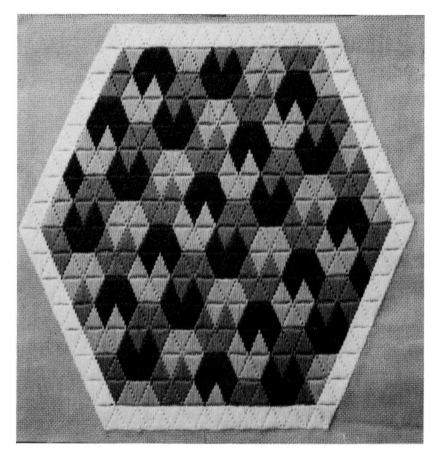

CLOUD PILLOW

COLOR PLATE	3
CANVAS:	#16
YARN COLORS:	4
FINISHED SIZE:	13¼″ × 13¼″

Practical

1. Starting at top left, stitch the first olive green reverse "S." The top and bottom of the reverse "S" are constructed of two hexagons from which one triangle has been extracted.
2. Stitch the medium faïence blue reverse "S" that lies to the bottom right and locks into the olive green "S."
3. Stitch the pale faïence blue reverse "S" that lies to the right of and locks into the lower half of the medium blue reverse "S."
   This sets your route.

Use

Pillow and, rescaled, floor cushion. Continuous field patterns that are cut off abruptly by their borders were an esteemed device of thirteenth- to sixteenth-century Turkish carpetmakers. I have read that such unending fields are meant to symbolize infinity or eternal life. That may be, but one wonders about the significance of the border that so cleanly and firmly cuts off these fields of eternity. Well, I, for one, do not propose to stitch "death" or its facsimile, so let us forget the whole matter. However, it is worth nothing that these continuous patterns are sociable and mass together much more satisfactorily than formal self-contained designs, which best occupy large areas of space—and frequently find close neighbors uncongenial. Designs of the first type, whether carpets or pillows, can be tossed together with happy abandon and enchanting results. Of course their colors must be sympathetic.

Source

French medieval mosaic. The S shapes resemble the cloud patterns used so frequently in the Middle and Far East.

Practical

1. Starting at top right, stitch the first blue half-hexagon. Then stitch the medium bronze diagonal rhombus to the left of the blue half-hexagon. (The rhombus slants from top left to bottom right.) Then stitch the blue hexagon to the left of the rhombus. Continue until reaching bottom.
2. Return to the top, stitch the light and deep bronze rhombuses to the left of the medium bronze rhombus. The deep tone is horizontal, the light tone is diagonal—slanting from top right to bottom left. With two needles, one threaded with the light and one with the deep tone of bronze, stitch the two rhombus forms in a diagonal row, leftward, to the bottom.
3. Return to the top, stitch the blue hexagon row again, and so forth.
4. If you want to emphasize the strapwork interlace, backstitch with very fine black yarn as shown in the upper half of the Color Plate. The lower half, not outlined, is more mellow, diffused. Backstitching should not be heavy, woolly, superimposed. It is meant here to become an integral part of the design, to define almost invisibly. It should not be a thick, vulgar addition or an obvious embroidered make-do solution to a construction problem in stitching or designing.

Use

Pillow and, rescaled, floor cushion, wall hanging, table carpet. If a border is desired, consider a deep blue, or brown (browns related to those in the field, but darker), or a pale ivory.

Source

Persian drawing, sixteenth century, in the British Museum, London. Also, the early twentieth-century Shaker cheese basket or any number of twelfth- and thirteenth-century architectural patterns left us by the Seljuks of Turkey and Persia.

PERSIAN BASKET

COLOR PLATE	4
CANVAS:	#16
YARN COLORS:	5
FINISHED SIZE:	15″ × 15″

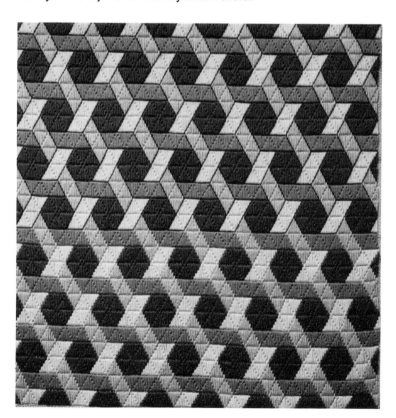

RED CUBES

Practical

1. Start at the right, at the top of the first vertical column of red cubes. Working with three needles, each threaded with one of the three tones of red required by this row, stitch the first vertical row of cubes.
2. Return to the top, stitch the second vertical row of cubes, to the left of the first row, and so forth.
3. Fill in the black background. Backgrounds are always stitched in the same trianglepoint as the design.

It is vital to follow the color gradations carefully to preserve the cubic form. You can reverse the tonal architecture so that the design is darkest at its outer edges and lightest at its center. In this event, you will require a light background.

Use

Pillow or telephone-directory cover. You can use tones of blue, green, or bronze-golds for the back of the cover, reds for the front. Rescale larger (#14 or #12 canvas) or multiply the *triangles* within the cubes (page 25) for a floor cushion, wall hanging, ceiling decoration. Use #18 or #20 canvas for smaller articles, and try silk yarn. The surface will look enameled.

Source

A fusion of medieval Islamic tiles, medieval mosaics in Venice, Palermo, and Florence, and nineteenth-century patchwork quilts.

COLOR PLATE	5
CANVAS:	#16
YARN COLORS:	11
FINISHED SIZE:	12½″ × 12½″

72

SNOW CRYSTAL KALEIDOSCOPE

Practical

1. Start with the three-toned bittersweet red hexagon in the middle of the canvas.
2. Stitch the blue points of the star. Continue the design, working hexagonal frame by hexagonal frame, until all are complete. Use two needles when the frames are in two colors.

Note that the radiating pale blue arms become increasingly lighter in tone as they near the outer frame.

Use

Pillow and, rescaled, floor cushion, wall hanging, ceiling design. The visual effect is that of a shimmering snow crystal or of a revolving, delicate spider-web wheel. Hexagons can be made into field patterns. See title page, for example.

Source

Original. Suggested by fifteenth-century Turkish carpets and twentieth-century kaleidoscopes.

Kaleidoscope designs in these hexagonal shapes make congenial and luminous companion pillows or floor cushions. If you wish to use them together, they will, of course, have to be worked in allied or harmonizing colors.

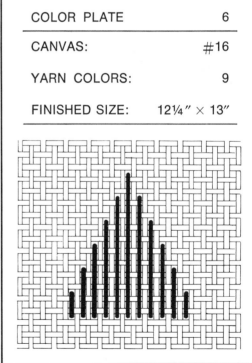

COLOR PLATE	6
CANVAS:	#16
YARN COLORS:	9
FINISHED SIZE:	12¼″ × 13″

Practical

Starting at top right, stitch the golden hexagonal frames until the canvas is covered. Fill in the **hexagonal** interiors bordered by these golden outlines with the white rhombuses and the black-pointed gold stars. Then fill in the **star-shaped** interiors formed by the golden outlines. Last of all, backstitch the **red** points of the stars with fine white yarn, and, with fine black yarn, the tiny black stars in the centers.

Use

Pillow, floor cushion, and, rescaled, table carpet, wall hanging, ceiling ornament. If a border is desired, the red of the star points, or a tone deeper, would be a good choice.

Source

Throne pattern from Persian miniature painting in *The Khamsa of Nizami,* "King Khusrau Seated upon His Throne," 1524, The Metropolitan Museum of Art, New York. I have retained its colors— the precious gold of the original yielding to mustard yarn. See photograph on page 16.

PERSIAN THRONE

COLOR PLATE	7
CANVAS:	#16
YARN COLORS:	5
FINISHED SIZE:	13" × 11½"

Practical

1. Starting at center top, stitch the large dark brown diamond, then the dark brown diamond immediately below.
2. Stitch one of the smaller cubes, starting at the center (the meeting point of the two dark brown diamonds).
3. After finishing the bronze cubes, stitch the steel gray surrounds. Finally, backstitch in very fine, very dark charcoal yarn. The Color Plate clearly shows the areas to be outlined. Do note that in cube designs no one side of a cube is ever in direct contact with a contiguous side that has the same tonal value. A light area is surrounded by medium and dark, medium by light and dark, dark by light and medium.

If you divide the composition vertically in half, you will see that one side reflects the rhombus forms of the other in an exact mathematical arrangement; it would be wise to take the time to understand it. If the underlying precept becomes known to you, it can be applied when making a new design or a variation of this one.

The tessellated bronze and steel rhombus forms make a cold, shimmering, polished surface that is counterbalanced by the warmth of the wool; this interplay of hot and cold is very interesting, and occurs in many of the trianglepoint designs.

Use

Pillow and, rescaled, wall hanging, floor cushion. The elongated hexagon is a pleasing shape for a pillow. See page 113. For a companion pillow or cushion, reverse the steel and bronze tones (steel-colored cubes in a bronze cubic frame). This design is an optical acrobat. Young children find invitation in its circus antics, and its irrepressible, constant motion and visual ambiguities are sophisticated enough for the adult mathematician.

Source

Based on the two top cubes of the wreath in Color Plate 12. The cubes have been broken up into the shaded rhombuses for sparkle.

COLOR PLATE	8
CANVAS:	#16

YARN COLORS: 10 bronzes, 2 dark browns, 7 steel grays, 1 very dark charcoal

FINISHED SIZE: 9″ × 14½″

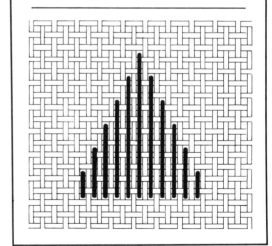

SHIMMERING DIAMONDS

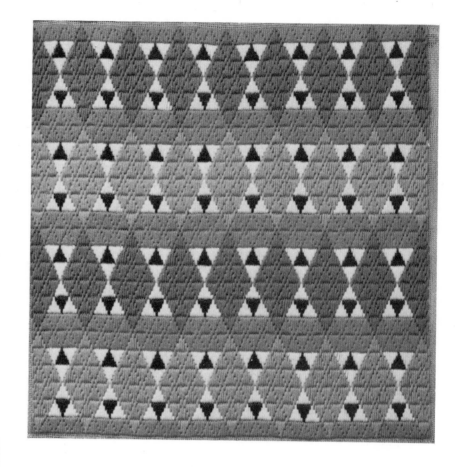

COLOR PLATE	9
CANVAS:	#16
YARN COLORS:	5
FINISHED SIZE:	12¾″ × 12¾″

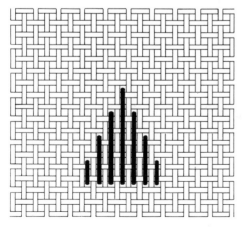

Practical

1. Starting at upper right, complete one horizontal row of the darker green diamonds. Return to the right and complete one horizontal row of the lighter green diamonds, and so forth, until all diamonds have been stitched.
2. Stitch the rows of lilac "ribbons."
3. Working with two needles, one threaded with white, the other with bottle green yarn, fill in the triangles between the diamonds.

Use

Pillow and, rescaled, floor cushion, wall hanging. The sparkling, lustrous surface seems to be a curious and fortunate characteristic of all 60-degree-angled mosaic designs; their visual appeal is as strong in wool as in the original medium, and equally suited to the wall. The pattern is also good turned on its side.

Source

Eleventh-century mosaic in the Santa Maria in Cosmedin, Rome, a very old church, of Greek origin; its original foundation dates back to the sixth century.

SHADOW BOXES

Practical

1. Starting at top right, stitch the first dark purple (zig) side of the box. The light and dark tones form a zigzag row.
2. Starting at the bottom left of the stitched dark purple (zig) side, stitch the light purple (zag) side. Continue the zigzag row of light purple and dark purple across the canvas. Always start the subsequent zag side from a point that is in contact with the previously stitched zig, to avoid having to count canvas threads.
3. Fill in the white diamonds as a last step.

Use

Pillow, floor cushion, and, rescaled larger, wall hanging. For a smaller pillow or for more frequent repeats of the pattern, use #18 or #20 canvas. As the stitches are lengthy, the work won't take long, even on very fine canvas. You can reverse the toning, using the darkest for the diamond interiors and the lightest for the zigs or zags.

Source

Patterns that simulate boxes, or intercutting slats, have been used by artisans of various disciplines in many countries and centuries, but not always in this 60-degree angle which contributes its own pronounced perspective; turned on its side, the pattern resembles a honeycomb.

COLOR PLATE	10
CANVAS:	#16
YARN COLORS:	3
FINISHED SIZE:	11″ × 12½″

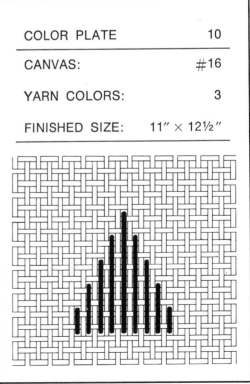

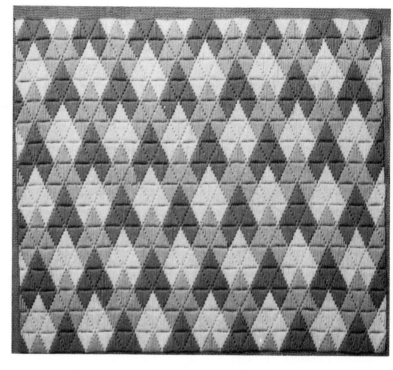

MOSAIC MITERS

COLOR PLATE	11
CANVAS:	#16
YARN COLORS:	3
FINISHED SIZE:	13″ × 14½″

Practical

1. Start at top right. Use two needles, one threaded with marigold yarn, one with orange yarn, and stitch the zigzag horizontal row, ending at the margin at the left. Return to the right, and repeat, until all marigold and orange zigzag rows have been completed.
2. Fill in the white forms between zigzags.

Use

Pillows and, rescaled, floor cushion, wall hanging. The design would also make a fine table carpet for a summer home in whatever garden shades meet the requirements of the environment. If so used, it will require a border, and for these particular colors I would suggest introducing a new color or tone for the border—a very deep burnt orange, splint basket brown, or soft medium violet. It is of interest that a majority of the great antique Islamic–oriental carpets of the thirteenth, fourteenth, fifteenth, and sixteenth centuries display a newly introduced color into the main border and sometimes into subsidiary borders. This acts as a chromatic refresher; the new colors in the borders also make the field pattern look raised, as though the carpet were resting on top of another carpet, or on a series of carpets, depending on the number of borders and the number of new tones. I have used this technique often in designing Oriental carpets and, on occasion, in this book. There are times we respond to a striking effect without quite seeing how it is achieved; luckily, there are also times, as with these carpet borders, when the technique is accessible to our understanding and application.

Source

Medieval French mosaic. Held at a distance, it resembles many Islamic tile patterns, its nature changing from angular to floral. When the eye isolates the forms in their vertical columns, the conical shapes seem to be overlapping miters: the tall caps with the high pointed arch that have given such visual excitement to ecclesiastical portraiture.

Practical

1. Start with the white star in the center.
2. Stitch the purple cubes surrounding the star, being careful to place the three tones correctly.
3. Stitch all the other cubes, each wreath in turn.
4. Stitch the white stars and the small white triangles and the white rows just within the frame.
5. Stitch the basket brown frame. Then split the brown yarn to make it thinner, and backstitch the stars.

You may wish to add a second border of lighter or deeper brown. Each wreath can be made of a different color, if you prefer, instead of four, as shown, or all can be made of various families of green: sage, olive, bottle, spring leaf, chartreuse, sea, emerald—using three tones, as shown. Or you can use one color, in three tones, for all. There are many color possibilities.

Use

Pillow and, rescaled, floor cushion, wall hanging, or ceiling design. This would be a good design, under lucite, for a hexagonal tray or small table top.

Source

Original. The shading of the cubes was suggested by an American pieced quilt, the Columbia Star.

WREATH KALEIDOSCOPE

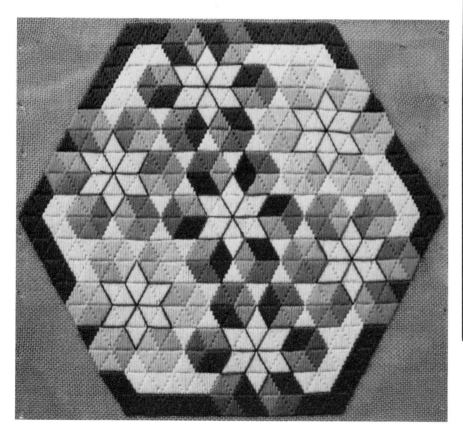

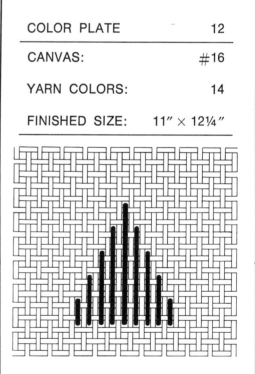

COLOR PLATE	12
CANVAS:	#16
YARN COLORS:	14
FINISHED SIZE:	11" × 12¼"

Practical

1. Starting near top center, stitch the navy blue six-footed (hexa-pod) wheel.
2. Diagonally below and to the left, stitch the red six-footed wheel that locks into the navy blue wheel.
3. Again, diagonally below, and to the left, stitch the white six-footed wheel that locks into the red wheel. Finish the row, return to the top, stitch the white wheel, and continue the diagonal interlocking row.

EGYPTIAN HEXAPOD

Use

Floor cushion, wall hanging, table carpet. For pillows of conventional size, also for book covers, tennis-racket covers, and so forth, #18 or #20 canvas should be used. This six-footed walking wheel probably represents the sun, as does its four-footed cousin, the fylfot cross (swastika); both are palpably charged with magical or religious energy. However we interpret or respond to their ancient and cross-cultural symbolism, they make dynamic geometric diaper patterns, employed frequently, effectively, and very individualistically in China, Japan, Egypt, Syria, Russia, Turkey, Venice, and Persia.

Source

The pattern is from a brass inlaid Egyptian pen case, fourteenth century.

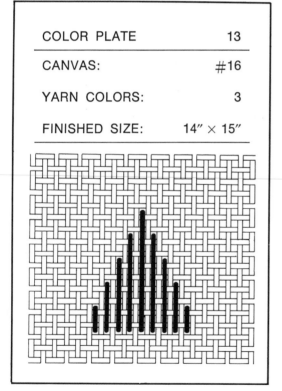

COLOR PLATE	13
CANVAS:	#16
YARN COLORS:	3
FINISHED SIZE:	14" × 15"

BLUE PERSIAN TILE

COLOR PLATE	14
CANVAS SIZE:	#16
YARN COLORS:	6
FINISHED SIZE:	13″ × 11″

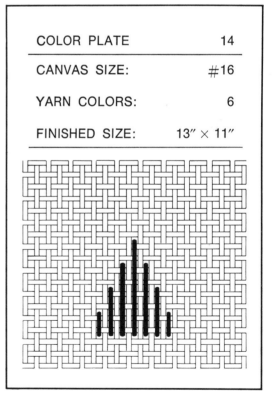

Practical

1. Stitch the white forms first (three hexagons in each). Work them in vertical rows, starting top right.
2. Fill in the blue hexagons, then outline the white forms with very fine, very dark charcoal gray backstitching.
3. Using subdued blue-green yarn, slightly heavier than the charcoal gray, backstitch the Y's (triskeles). Each arm of the Y enters one white hexagon.
4. Stitch **One** horizontal row of the top border, immediately above the field pattern. This single black row provides the base for the ribbon border, all four sides of which can now be completed. Fill in remainder of the black border.

Use

Pillow and, rescaled, floor cushion, wall hanging, table carpet. This pillow is a great favorite among my friends, many of whom would like to make it as a carpet—for which use the long stitch is unsuitable, because it would not withstand the severe abuse to which such a function would subject it. One adventurer is, nevertheless, proceeding on #16 canvas, using more stitches to increase the size of the *triangle;* he will have an excellent table carpet or wall hanging to grace his floor.

Source

Field from Persian miniature painting, "Iskandar in a Magic Garden," 1435, the Chester Beatty Library, Dublin. I have chosen a border that derives from Turkish and Persian carpets of the same period. This three-dimensional ribbon pattern was also favored by Byzantine mosaic artisans, who used it in Ravenna and other great centers of Byzantium, to adorn the splendidly tessellated floors, ceilings, and walls of their cathedrals and chapels.

See photograph on page 17.

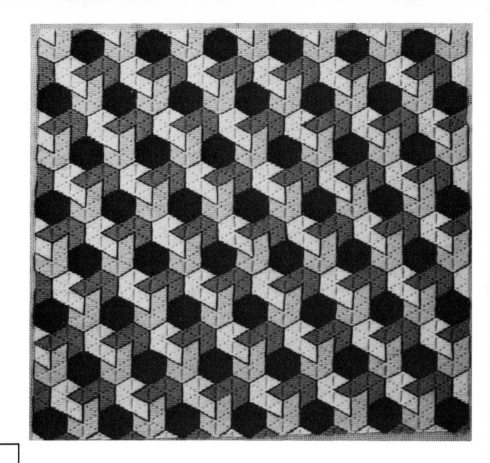

PERSIAN CARPET KNOTS

COLOR PLATE	15
CANVAS:	#16
YARN COLORS:	4
FINISHED SIZE:	12¼″ × 13¼″

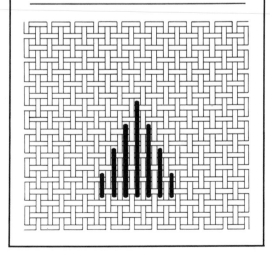

Practical

1. Starting near top right, working with three needles, each threaded with one of the three tones of the "knots," stitch the first "knot" (complete), then the second, below to its left. The third "knot" is immediately below the second, on the left. The fourth "knot" is immediately below the third, on the left. This sets the route. Finish all the diagonal rows constructed of these three-toned "knots," filling in incomplete knots at the end.
2. Fill in all the charcoal brown hexagons.
3. Backstitch the "knots," as clearly shown in the Color Plate, with extremely fine yarn, the same color as the hexagons.

Use

This is a mysteriously interesting pattern, one that is useful for small articles (#18 or #20 canvas), such as eyeglass cases, slippers, playing-card box tops, and so forth. Rescaled larger than shown (#14 canvas, additional stitches in the *triangle*), it will make a Persian palace mosaic floor cushion or table carpet. As shown (#16 canvas), it is appropriate for a pillow, tennis-racket cover, telephone-directory cover.

Source

From a carpet pattern in the Turkish miniature painting "Taking Away of Jam-i-Jihannūma," sixteenth century, Topkapi Saray Museum, Istanbul. See photograph on page 29. The miniaturists were fastidious observers and faithful renderers of the furnishings of their period, and I think we can assume such a carpet existed. Also, a tile pattern in the Persian miniature painting in the *Shahnama,* "Bahrum Gur Entertaining Shangul of Hind," 1560, India Office Library.

Practical

1. Stitch the bronze leaf first, starting with its palest hexagon in the upper right corner. Stitch all the other leaves from the **center,** working the **darkest** hexagon first and graduating lighter toward the border. Work each leaf in turn.
2. Stitch the pearly gray-white center hexagon, in the middle of the canvas. Continue the grays, working outward, in successively deepening tones, ending with the border of charcoal. This cross-current of tones, the grays being light at the center and darkening toward the border, the leaves dark at the center and lightening toward the border, is responsible for the striking luminosity of the surface.
3. The backstitches at the center, and in the six angles of the frame, use yarn of the same color and weight as that of the hexagons to which they are attached.

Use

Pillow and, rescaled, floor cushion, wall hanging, ceiling decoration. You can make this sexfoil design larger by increasing the number of hexagon rows within the leaves, simultaneously increasing the number of yarn tones. The colors are: bronzes, olive greens, ash violets, ginger browns, taupe-fawns, soft blue-greens. Ombré toning, such as that used here or in Hungarian point (bargello) or flame stitch, intensifies hue so dramatically that I prefer to use subdued, tender, nonvibrant colors. This is a matter of taste.

Source

Original. Based on a pattern in my do-it-yourself kaleidoscope into which I had placed some light and dark raisins, some bits of almonds and pistachios, and a few whole-wheat Italian bread crumbs.

LIGHTS AND SHADOWS KALEIDOSCOPE

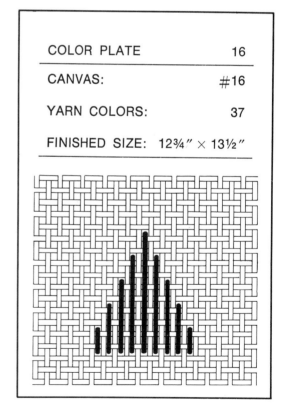

COLOR PLATE	16
CANVAS:	#16
YARN COLORS:	37
FINISHED SIZE:	12¾″ × 13½″

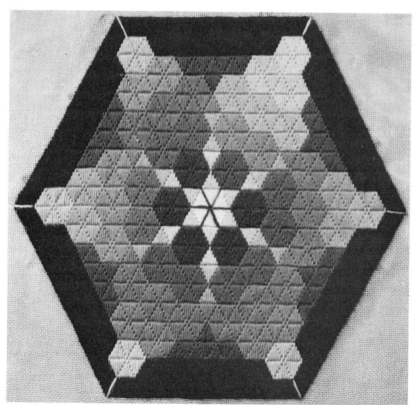

Practical

1. Start at top right, or left, and stitch the navy blue horizontal zig-zag line across the canvas. This establishes the route.
2. Stitch the deep turquoise-green zigzag row immediately below.
3. Using two needles, one threaded with medium turquoise-green yarn, the other with white yarn, stitch the rhombus forms in the zigzag row immediately below.
4. Continue to work the zigzag rows in identical fashion, using two needles wherever two colors appear in one row.

Please note that all colors, except the navy and the white, are present in two shades: two ginger browns, two turquoise-greens, two soft, light olive greens. The Color Plate shows clearly which tone is used for which row. If you feel the repeats occur at too great a distance, you can eliminate some of the rows, but I advise caution: this is a very clever design! Use #18 or #20 canvas if you want more repeats to show. The colors can be changed, of course, but be faithful to the chromatic architecture.

Use

Pillow, floor cushion, and, rescaled, table carpet, ceiling decoration, wall hanging—the last, in my opinion, the most exciting. This design is geometric sorcery and has many marvels and curiosities to reveal when viewed from different distances and angles. Its unique characteristics are no less spellbinding when the design is turned on its side.

Source

I have changed the colors, but the pattern and toning are from an early medieval mosaic, San Marco Cathedral, Venice.

ADRIATIC WAVES

COLOR PLATE	17
CANVAS:	#16
YARN COLORS:	8
FINISHED SIZE:	15½″ × 15½″

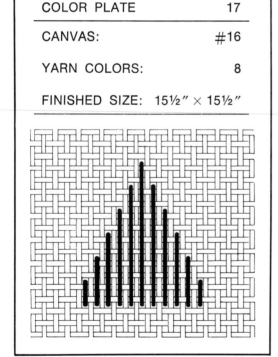

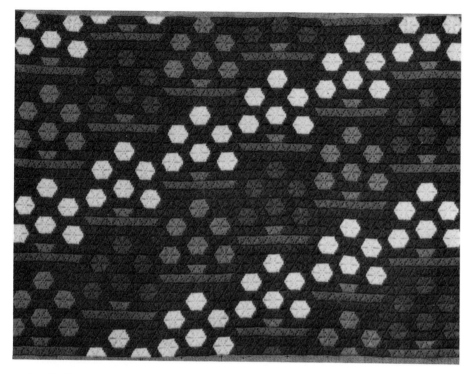

FROISSART WALL HANGING
(DETAIL)

Practical

1. Starting at top right, stitch the white blossom spray, surround it with the green background, stitch the "vase" below, continue to the next white blossom spray, diagonally down and leftward. The top part of the "vase" is slightly lighter than the bottom.
2. Work the red and the blue blossom sprays, following the diagonal route, and filling in background and "vases" as you go. This last is to save counting tiny canvas threads or squares in order to place the sprays.

Use

Sofa throw. Wall hanging. These proportions are meant to hang above a bed. (Color Plate 1—the painting—shows the design lengthened.) Four vertical rows of the sprays make a fine pillow; six make a floor cushion. Rescaled a bit larger (same canvas, but increase the number of stitches in the *triangle*), it would make a splendid table carpet.

Source

This is a slightly simplified, less naturalistic adaptation of a wall hanging in the illuminated manuscript, *The Chronicles of Froissart,* fifteenth-century France, the British Museum, London. See Color Plate 1. The paintings in *The Chronicles* exhibit an extraordinary variety of wall hangings which, to my eye, appear to be meticulous and accurate paintings of contemporaneous European and Persian textile designs. And what splendid hangings they are! One glance at them, or at other paintings and illuminated manuscripts of the period, should certainly destroy the notion that "Middle Ages" stands for gloomy, dusty, depressing colors. On the contrary, its palette is as clear and as joyous as that of Matisse. Children know this. They have always been drawn to the sunny, unshadowed pigments of this brilliant era of palaces and kings, and heraldic shields, and harlequins in motley, and jauntily caparisoned horses. Adults forget. No doubt they have seen too many moldy sets in too many pseudo-Gothic horror movies. Let us discard the romantic, eerie trappings. The reality is more inviting.

COLOR PLATE	18
CANVAS SIZE:	#16
YARN COLORS:	6
FINISHED SIZE:	17" × 49"

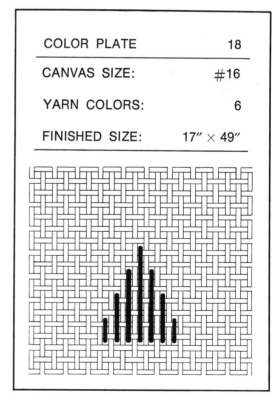

SNOW FLOWERS

COLOR PLATE	19
CANVAS:	#16
YARN COLORS:	16
FINISHED SIZE:	13¾″ × 15¾″

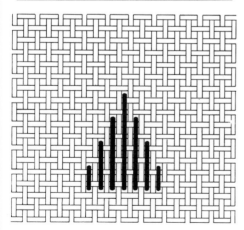

Practical

1. At top right, stitch the three light blue hexagons and the two light blue half-hexagons that make the incomplete first flower.
2. Descending diagonally leftward, complete the row of flowers. Stitch all the other flowers in the same route, from top to bottom.
3. Fill in the two-toned star centers, and the black *triangles* that form the background.

Use

Pillow and floor cushion. The flowers appear to be strewn at random, but there is a repeat every fourth row. Using isometric graph paper, you can work them into a more regulated, formal composition and, if you rescale larger, the flowers, thus arranged, should make a fine wall hanging, floor cushion, or table carpet.

Source

Pieced quilt, c. 1880, the American Museum, Bath, England. Two American men, reversing the usual cultural travelogue, assembled an exceptionally fine collection of American eighteenth- and nineteenth-century urban and rural furnishings; they placed it in Bath, where it offers a unique education in American cultural habits as reflected by styles of environment, furnishings, tools, and domestic utensils. See photograph on page 18. Also see the snow crystal photograph on page 10.

PALERMO MEANDER

Practical

It should be noted that the design is constructed of half-stars that descend from top left rightward; an examination of the Color Plate will show clearly that the white and medium-violet half-stars always point upward; the olive green and light lilac half-stars point upward one row, downward the next. Work the half-stars, color by

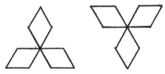

color, in diagonal rows, starting at top left, descending to the right, to establish the route.

Use

A dazzler, the stars, cubes, and diamonds participate in a joyous and perplexing interplay; the continuous, sinuous movement is highly organized, thus avoiding restlessness.

Pillow, floor cushion, and, rescaled, table carpet, wall hanging. If you feel like presenting yourself with a Persian pavilion floor, make a group of floor cushions. You can achieve variety and harmony by changing the tonal values in this design (for quite different effects) and by adding more cushions, in kindred colors, based on the variations of this pattern in the Sketchbook, Drawings 20a and 20b.

Source

Norman–Moorish mosaic, the Cappella of San Pietro, eleventh century, Palermo, Sicily.

COLOR PLATE	20
CANVAS:	#16
YARN COLORS:	4
FINISHED SIZE:	14″ × 15″

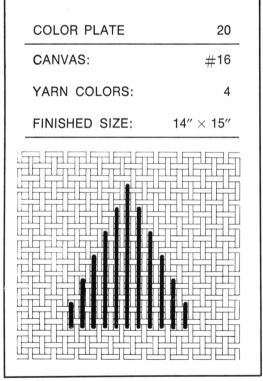

Practical

1. Stitch all the red hexagonal frames—they are constructed of double rows of *triangles.*
2. Fill in the blue and olive green centers, then backstitch the red hexagons with slightly lighter-weight white yarn.
3. Stitch the bright heraldic emerald green and white border. Finally, with very fine black yarn, backstitch where border meets field pattern.

Use

Pillow and, rescaled, floor cushion, wall hanging, table carpet. Navy blue and white, or crimson and white, or cobalt blue and black are also good choices for the exhilarating stripes of the border. Of course, the field colors will have to be adjusted accordingly.

Source

Field adapted from Persian miniature painting, "Siyawah Tempted by Sudaba," 1446, the British Museum, London. The border is typical of those to be found in contemporaneous Islamic miniatures, and its vigorous, clean stripe is probably the precursor of the canopy or awning.

TURKISH TENT

COLOR PLATE	21
CANVAS:	#16
YARN COLORS:	7
FINISHED SIZE:	14½″ × 12″

HARLEQUIN CUBE

Practical

1. Starting at top center, stitch the first oyster gray diamond (two *triangles* on their sides). Use up the strand of yarn by stitching a few additional oyster gray diamonds in a diagonal row.
2. Immediately under the center oyster gray diamond, start the rhombuses belonging to the right side of the cubic frame. Finish this side and proceed to the small center cube or continue to work the large cubic frame. The three-dimensional effect is maintained, as mentioned in connection with previous cubic designs, by keeping the sides of the cubes from surrounds of the same tonal value. Here, the sides of the inner cube consist of rhombuses in (1) light bright, (2) medium bright, (3) somber tones. An inspection will show you that (1) light bright tone is neighbored by (2) medium bright, and (3) somber, and so forth.

Use

Pillow and, rescaled larger, wall hanging, floor cushion.

Source

This and the two designs that follow have been inspired by the paintings of Victor Vasarely. Of course, I have changed many colors, the geometric shapes, the scale of the forms, and the medium. I have always stood opposed to the use of paintings for needlepoint work, feeling that such transference undermined and perverted the art of the first and failed to use the unique and respectable characteristics of the second. But some modern optical art, in its firm geometric structure, seems to me adaptable. Needlepoint transforms it, for personal use; it changes without imposing injury on the original concept.

COLOR PLATE	22
CANVAS:	#14
YARN COLORS:	26
FINISHED SIZE:	10½″ × 11¼″

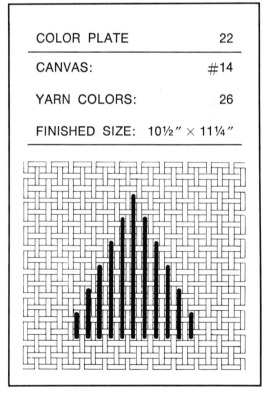

TRANSILIENT PRISMS WALL HANGING

COLOR PLATE	23
CANVAS:	#16
YARN COLORS:	11 blues, 4 violets, 2 lilacs, 7 greens, 2 blue-greens, 2 rusts, 3 grays, 3 scarlets, 3 browns, 1 black
FINISHED SIZE:	51″ × 21½″

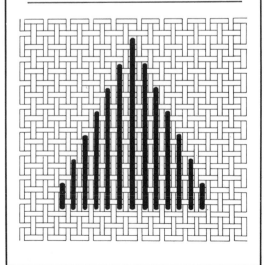

Practical

1. Start at center top and stitch the first cube. Stitch the three cubes directly below in a vertical row.
2. Stitch the three cubes to the right of the center four, starting at the top.
3. Stitch the three cubes to the left of the center four.
4. Stitch the black background.

Make certain that the yarn covers the canvas adequately. I prefer a smooth surface for the trianglepoint canvas patterns and, to my eye, a little canvas peeking through is less destructive of geometric design than fuzzy bulk. Dark yarns tend to be thinner than light yarns. If you are working with dark yarn that can be split (Persian, Nantucket worsted), add one single strand to compensate. If not, and the peek-through of canvas threads is disturbing, daub and patch tenderly and judiciously with **indelible waterproof** markers in the matching colors. **Always** test your marker by applying it to paper and immersing the paper in water. I have had occasion to use this technique of first aid only once, for black, and it worked admirably. If you lay your stitches carefully, with yarn flat and untensed, it should not be necessary.

Use

Wall hanging. For a pillow, #18 or #20 canvas can be used. Silk yarn would be very effective on the finer canvas. Of course, the design would be used on its side for a pillow or, for that matter, a wall hanging if you prefer it that way. I am now stitching this in vibrant autumn tones, shot with brilliant reds, oranges, golds. And I would very much like to see it in burnished metallic colors: bronzes, steels, silvers, irons, golds, pewters. Working this has taught me much about the architecture of color. As each rhombus, in a different color or tone, entered the arena, a startling metamorphosis occurred; much as in chess, every additional move seemed to affect all the relationships on the ground. This instructive and engrossing transilience continued throughout and made the work entertaining.

Source

See preceding design, Harlequin Cube, page 89.

Practical

1. Start with the two blue cubes in the center, stitching either one, then stitch the second. Complete the mauve cube and the chartreuse cube.
2. Stitch the surround, which is divided asymmetrically around the cubes, using black and two deeper tones of the colors employed in the cubes. Note that I arranged the deeper tones of the frame in diametric opposition to the lighter-toned cubes: the mauve cube is bordered by greens, the chartreuse cube is bordered by mauves, the indigo blue cube is bordered by hyacinth blues, and the hyacinth blue cube is bordered by indigo blues.

Use

Wall hanging, floor cushion (several with different-colored cubes would make a spectacularly bejeweled floor). Use #18 canvas for pillows; silk yarn would bring a marvelous polished surface to the fine canvas. Rescale larger for ceiling "meteors" (#12 canvas).

Source

See Harlequin Cube, page 89.

CRYSTAL WALL HANGING

COLOR PLATE	24
CANVAS:	#16

YARN COLORS: Border—12, cubes—16 (4 for each cube)

FINISHED SIZE: 20¾″ × 19½″

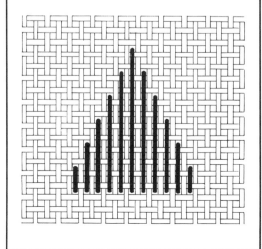

TURKISH SKY

COLOR PLATE	25
CANVAS:	#16
YARN COLORS:	3
FINISHED SIZE:	9½″ × 10¾″

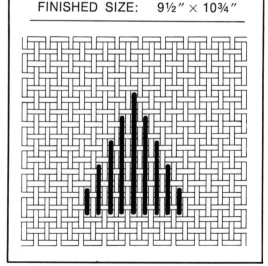

Practical

1. Starting at top right, stitch one horizontal row of incomplete blue stars. Work the darker blue points (triangles) first, then the medium blue centers (hexagons). Complete all the stars, always working in horizontal rows and always stitching the points first.
2. Fill in the white rhombus forms, working horizontally or diagonally.
3. Backstitch, with slightly finer white yarn, the small star in the center of the hexagon, using the perforations made by previous stitching. If you consult the Color Plate, you will observe that one such star, at upper right, has been left incomplete so that its construction can be easily observed.

Use

Pillow and, rescaled, floor cushion, wall hanging, table carpet, ceiling decoration. The small white stars, the blue stars, and the hexagonally shaped white frames appear to be engaged in a struggle to dominate the surface, each attempting to lay claim to the foreground. This receding and emerging, shifting domination seems to involve the eye in an unending Sisyphean activity, producing a very animated and entertaining pattern.

Source

Turkish *malakari* (colored plaster work) ceiling, Muradiye Cemetery, 1426, Bursa, Turkey. Also tile design, Persian miniature painting, "Muhammad Seated Among Companions," c. 1485, the Bodleian Library, Oxford, England.

See photograph on page 27.

PIECED QUILT TURKISH SKY

COLOR PLATE	26
FINISHED SIZE:	22″ × 23″

The three fabrics (two blue and one white) were cut into equilateral triangles, each side measuring 2½ inches; then they were placed together in the exact arrangement of the stitched *triangles* on canvas. Trianglepoint has such close affinity with the structural techniques of patchwork piecing (which itself uses the technique of mosaic) that the joining here of all three media seems both justified and inevitable. Most of the designs in the book derive from medieval Islamic and European architecture, tile work, floor and wall mosaics, wall hangings, and they were created by the supreme masters of geometric ornamentation. The clean dignity and iridescent mystery of these diaper patterns made wondrous interiors in the past; their structure, functional nature, and scale are similarly ideal for patchwork quilts—whether for bed or wall—and I very much regret that space and time do not allow further examples here. I hope, meager offering notwithstanding, that these stitched designs and those in the sketchbook will be used as a source for the pieced quilt—a form of mosaic work made from fabric.

Turkish Sky, pieced-quilt sample stitched by Barbara Cooke.

SOLAR KALEIDOSCOPE

Practical

1. Starting at top center, stitch the arm of golden diamonds that radiates from the top point of the star, then stitch the star, then the five other radiating golden arms.
2. It will be seen that six radiating arms divide the canvas into six pie-shaped wedges and that these wedges house small three-toned cubes. Complete each wedge individually, starting from the star and following the shading arrangement of cubes in each wedge.
3. The outer edges of the design maintain the same tonal system. However, the lightest shade of the cube is replaced by the medium, the medium by the dark, and the dark by a newly introduced darker tone of the same color family.

Use

This makes a most interesting mosaiclike floor cushion and, re-scaled, wall hanging and ceiling decoration. The tones of bronze, here used, give the effect of marquetry or parquet; other tones will bring surprises. It would even be possible to use a different color family for each wedge, in a spectrum arrangement.

Source

Original.

COLOR PLATE	27
CANVAS:	#14
YARN COLORS:	5
FINISHED SIZE:	19¾″ × 22½″

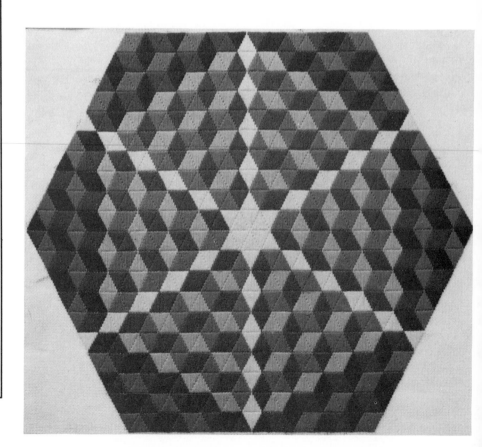

94

STAINED GLASS KALEIDOSCOPE

Practical

1. Start with the three green and the three white *triangles* that form the hexagonal center of the star; then stitch the six navy blue points of the star and the navy blue *triangles* that touch these points.
2. Moving outward from the star, stitch the red surround, then the six green stars, and so forth.
3. After field and border have been completed, outline the stars, rhombuses, and other figures with medium-fine black yarn as shown in the Color Plate.

A word about the backstitching: In general, I prefer the finest possible yarn to outline these geometric shapes—the yarn should delineate the contours modestly, without presenting itself as a separate, noticeable element. However, medium-fine yarn (just slightly lighter in weight than that used to compose the design) here acts as a substitute for the lead in stained glass, and, in this case, it should be prominent.

Use

Pillow and, rescaled, wall hanging, floor cushion, ceiling decoration. The colors used are those of medieval stained-glass panels, but the design can be worked in any other compatible color group, such as: pastel, subdued, autumn. Can be made into field pattern. See title page.

Source

Original. A fusion of fifteenth-century Turkish carpets and twentieth-century kaleidoscopes.

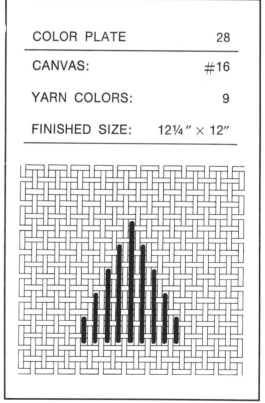

COLOR PLATE	28
CANVAS:	#16
YARN COLORS:	9
FINISHED SIZE:	12¼″ × 12″

SNOWCAPS

COLOR PLATE	29
CANVAS:	#16
YARN COLORS:	3
FINISHED SIZE:	12¼″ × 12½″

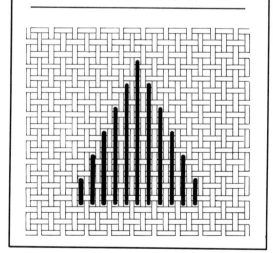

Practical

Start at top right and work the "caps" in a vertical row. Complete the design by working all the vertical rows in the same manner. Two or four colors can be used rather than three. Different colors can be used every other row. The rhythm of the design depends on the placement of the colors, and many variations and tonal treatments are possible.

Use

Pillow, floor cushion, and, rescaled and with some further color experiment, wall hanging. For a conventional small pillow I would reduce the number of stitches within the basic *triangle;* this will allow increased repeats and the pattern will emerge more satisfactorily.

Source

Woven shawl, nineteeth century, the Sandwich Islands.

SELJUK BRICK

Practical

1. At top right, stitch the light brown area of the partially completed "Y," then stitch the medium brown vertical area immediately below the light brown.
2. Continue in a vertical row, downward, stitching first the light brown, then the medium brown areas of the "Y"s. Return to the top, repeat until all these brown forms are complete.
3. Fill in the white areas.
4. Fill in the dark brown triangles.

Use

Pillow, floor cushion (slightly larger scale), wall hanging (larger scale). A very good design for a tray—under a layer of lucite (#18 or #20 canvas)—or a footstool. A friend is making a rather sizable piece to be tossed over the back of a brown velvet sofa; it will replace a frayed-beyond-redemption Oriental carpet. In these tones the pattern is particularly happy with baskets, bamboo, pewter, copper, but many color combinations are possible.

Source

Seljuk brick pattern, arch of the Kharraqan tomb tower, 1067, western Iran. See photograph on page 19. The two towers that remain show seventy-odd patterns, surely an immoderate, exhibitionistic display—that is, in hands other than those of the Seljuks, whose sensitivity to order and refinement never failed, and whose arrangements, no matter how exuberant and varied, never suggest ostentation.

COLOR PLATE	30
CANVAS:	#16
YARN COLORS:	4
FINISHED SIZE:	11″ × 12¼″

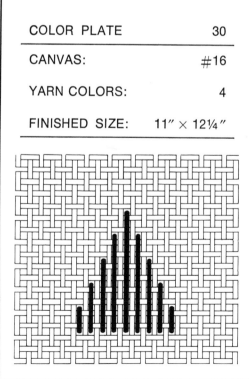

WHIRLING HEXAGONS

COLOR PLATE	31
CANVAS:	#16
YARN COLORS:	4
FINISHED SIZE:	14″ × 13½″

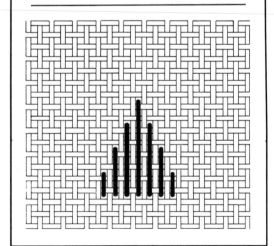

Practical

1. Start at top right, work the two-toned hexagonal frames (three pale and three deep copper red triangles) in a diagonal row, descending leftward. Finish all the red triangles.
2. Fill in the green hexagons within the red frames.
3. Fill in the medium indigo blue background. Indigo is the slightly greened medium or dark blue (close to navy) commonly used for the unsurpassable Flemish medieval tapestries and for the great early Turkish and Persian carpets. It knows no equal as an enhancer of its fellow colors. I have never been truly attracted to a carpet that did not use it in some form, however gently or minutely. It is, for me, an essential ingredient of the Oriental carpet and is in good part responsible for its jewel-like surface.

Use

Pillow (change to #18 or #20 canvas for a small pillow or for increased repeats of the pattern), floor cushion and, rescaled, wall hanging, table carpet. The indigo or the green (same tones or a little deeper) can be used for a border color. The triangles can be worked in one color only, in which case backstitch-outline them with fine black yarn to preserve their contours.

Source

A great favorite of the Persian miniaturists, the pattern can be seen as a tile in *The Khamsa of Nizami,* "Fitna Carrying the Cow Upstairs to Bahram Gur," 1481, the Chester Beatty Library, Dublin, and in the manuscript, *Majālis Al-Ushāq,* "The Poet Jalal ad-Dīn," 1552, the Bodleian Library, Oxford, England.

Practical

1. Starting below star, top right, stitch the first **completed diagonal** two-toned green "bar." This "bar" slants from top left to bottom right. Then stitch the diagonal "bar" that is its immediate neighbor to the left. This "bar" slants from top right to bottom left. Continue these "bars" across the canvas. They make one zigzag row.
2. Stitch the two-toned green **horizontal** "bars" immediately above and below the zigzag "bars." Then stitch the second zigzag row. Complete all the green "bars" in this way.
3. Stitch the dark green and white stars.
4. Stitch the red triangles (each triangle consists of four basic *triangles*).

Use

Pillow and, rescaled, floor cushion, table carpet, wall hanging, ceiling design. The same red, or a shade deeper, of the triangles can be used for a border. If this border is made sufficiently large, the green and white stars can be used as a motif within the border. Work this out on isometric graph paper.

Source

Original. Suggested by many similarly structured designs in Persian and Turkish miniature paintings and Seljuk architecture. See Sketchbook, Drawings 13, 14.

STARRED HONEYCOMB

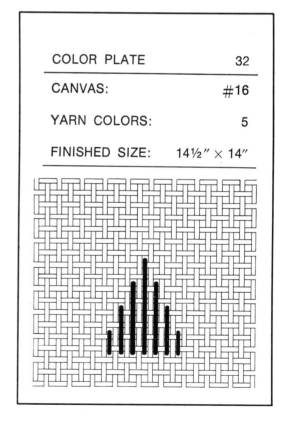

COLOR PLATE	32
CANVAS:	#16
YARN COLORS:	5
FINISHED SIZE:	14½″ × 14″

BUSBY BERKELEY'S STARS

Practical

1. Start with the center golden star (note the two tones of yarn, please).
2. Stitch the six white diamonds that touch the six points of the central star. Stitch the six stars that touch the points of the six white diamonds. Finish all white diamonds.
3. Stitch the red bars that radiate out from the stars.
4. Stitch the royal blue bars.
5. Backstitch the forms with very fine golden yarn, following the outlines, as shown in the Color Plate.

Use

Pillow, floor cushion, and, rescaled, table carpet, ceiling ornament, wall hanging.

Source

It is said that the ancient Persian rulers found recreation in gaming with living men on giant chessboards. How they would have delighted in the Human Kaleidoscope—a spectacular, astonishing toy devised by the brilliant geometric genie, Busby Berkeley, who is the begetter of this design. I have taken the liberty of substituting rhombuses and triangles for arms and legs, and stars for golden tresses. This great mathematical fantasist saw the populace, as did his predecessors, the eccentric and superb Romanesque painters of the twelfth century, as linear elements in a magnificent geometric layout. This paradox of his work is arresting: he reduces the human form to the abstract patterns of inanimate objects, but his choreography reanimates and heightens it to living myth.

The design is also suggestive of the eight-pointed so-called effulgent stars that figure prominently in the Spanish–Moorish carpets of the fifteenth and sixteenth centuries.

COLOR PLATE	33
CANVAS:	#16
COLORS:	5
FINISHED SIZE:	12¼″ × 13¾″

100

SUNBURST KALEIDOSCOPE

Practical

1. Start with the deep bronze star in the center.
2. Stitch the white surround of the star.
3. Stitch the one-shade-lighter bronze surround. Continue to stitch the white and the bronze surrounds as shown in the Color Plate.

You can reverse the tonal scheme by stitching the center star in the lightest bronze-gold and radiating out in darker bronze tones. You can also change the white to black for a modern, brilliant surface. Black might be combined with tones of cobalt blues or coppery reds.

You can also use several colors, or use tones that do not necessarily graduate in regular sequence.

Use

Pillow and, rescaled a *little* larger (use more stitches for the *triangle* or #14 canvas), floor cushion. Rescale considerably larger for a wall hanging or ceiling decoration. All these hexagonally shaped designs can be converted to rectangles by continuing the pattern to right-angled corners. Or you can build a rectangular surround in a contrasting color—in this case, rich mahogany brown, perhaps, or deep pewter, or deep Venetian red. Or turn it into a Star of Bethlehem; see Sketchbook, Drawing 2.

Source

Twelfth-century church window, St. Denis, France, and pieced American patchwork quilt called Sunburst, this last much sought after by collectors because it makes a vibrant, exhilarating wall hanging . . . as it can in trianglepoint. See related quilt on page 18.

COLOR PLATE	34
CANVAS:	#16
YARN COLORS:	6
FINISHED SIZE:	14″ × 14¾″

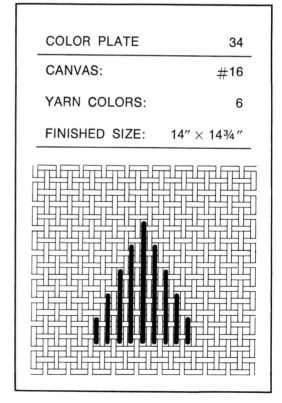

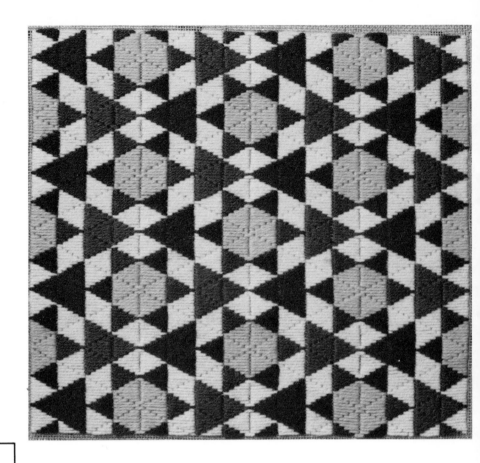

STARS WITHIN STARS

COLOR PLATE	35
CANVAS:	#14
YARN COLORS:	6
FINISHED SIZE:	10½″ × 9½″

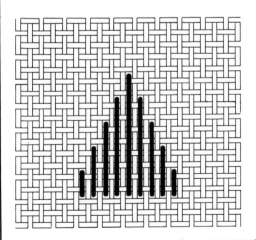

Practical

An inspection of the photograph will reveal that there is a white hexagon frame (composed of six rhombus forms) that lies within the six points of the larger star. Starting at center top, work the first complete white hexagonal frame, then those that fall below in a vertical column. This sets the pattern, and you can continue to work these vertical white columns—or to complete the inner and/or outer stars as you proceed. Note the two tones of ash lilac and the two tones of bottle green used for the star points. This lends iridescence.

Use

Pillow, floor cushion, and, rescaled, table carpet, wall hanging, or ceiling decoration. This design is disingenuous, its seeming structural simplicity misleading; it does not reveal its kaleidoscopic secrets all at once. It is one of the most generous and fascinating of all mosaic patterns. Long viewing brings many curious configurations and variations.

Source

Twelfth-century mosaic, San Marco Cathedral, Venice.

CAMERA OBSCURA

Practical

1. Starting at top right, stitch the first light blue horizontal rhombus. Immediately below and to the left, stitch the vertical (slanted) light blue rhombus. Immediately below, and to the left, stitch the next light blue horizontal rhombus. Complete all the light rhombus forms, always starting from the top and maintaining the stepped descent described above.
2. Stitch the smaller deep turquoise-green rhombus forms that complete the frames of the "chambers."
3. Stitch the interiors of the "chambers," working with three needles, one threaded with one of the two shades of the emerald green, one threaded with the other green, and the third threaded with the deep charcoal gray.
4. Outline the forms, as shown in the Color Plate, by backstitching with very fine black yarn.

Use

Pillow and, rescaled, floor cushion, wall hanging, ceiling design.

Source

Medieval mosaic, San Marco Cathedral, Venice. Very similar designs were frequently used in Byzantine mosaic ceilings which, seen from below, give the viewer the impression of peering up into compartments of immense depths.

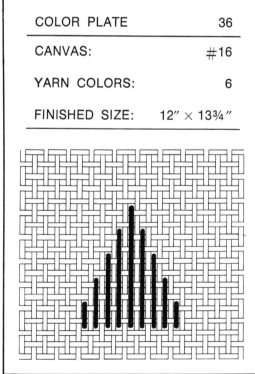

COLOR PLATE	36
CANVAS:	#16
YARN COLORS:	6
FINISHED SIZE:	12″ × 13¾″

GRANDMOTHER'S FLOWER GARDEN

COLOR PLATE	37
CANVAS:	#14
YARN COLORS:	3
FINISHED SIZE:	12¾" × 11½"

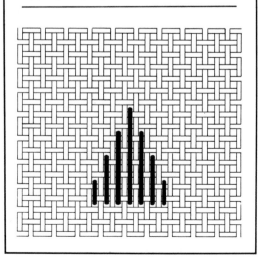

Practical

1. Stitch the green hexagons first, starting at top right and working left in a horizontal zigzag row. Return to right, stitch the green hexagon that connects the two horizontal zigzag rows. Continue these horizontal zigzag rows, always filling in the connecting hexagon, until all have been stitched.
2. Stitch the white hexagons, flower by flower.
3. Fill in the gold hexagon centers.

Use

Pillow (for a smaller pillow or more repeats, use #18 or #20 canvas), floor cushion, and, rescaled larger, table carpet, wall hanging. The flowers can be made in varying colors—for instance, pale violets, lilacs, pinks, blues. The central hexagon can be brown, black, or whatever other color you select. If you use the finer canvas (#20), one or two hexagonal frames can be added, in different floral tones, to the white one. Each frame will, of course, grow proportionately.

Source

This much-used Persian and Turkish tile pattern was given an affectionate revival by nineteenth- and twentieth-century American and English patchwork quilt artisans; the scraps of the sewing basket were recruited to make an exuberant prismatic garden. The very frugality that found a practical use for the motley bits of fabric was responsible for the parti-colored charm of the Grandmother's Flower Garden patchwork quilt.

Practical

1. Stitch the complete pinwheel near top right.
2. Surround it with the bright navy blue background.
3. Stitch the pinwheel immediately below and to the left of the first pinwheel. Continue in this diagonal descent, stitching the background every time a pinwheel is complete. This saves you from having to count tiny canvas squares to place the pinwheels.

Use

Pillow, floor cushion, table carpet, wall hanging, ceiling decoration. For a smaller pillow or one showing more repeats, use fewer stitches in the *triangle;* see the photograph above for example. See foot of Color Plate for example of color alteration. This design would, I think, be extremely effective in whites and various pale pearly grays on black. The pinwheels will look like sparkling snow crystals on a night ground.

Source

The pinwheel is taken from the Sirçali *medrese,* a secondary, sometimes theological, school, where it can be seen, as part of a more intricate pattern, in blue and black enameled brickwork, c. 1243, Konya. *Medrese* is the Turkish spelling, *madrasa* the Persian.

SELJUK PINWHEELS

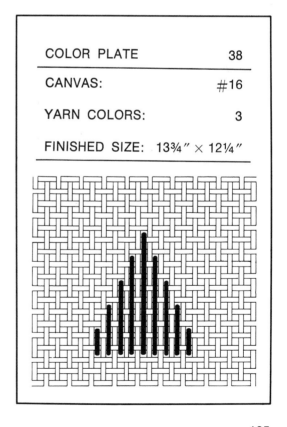

COLOR PLATE	38
CANVAS:	#16
YARN COLORS:	3
FINISHED SIZE:	13¾″ × 12¼″

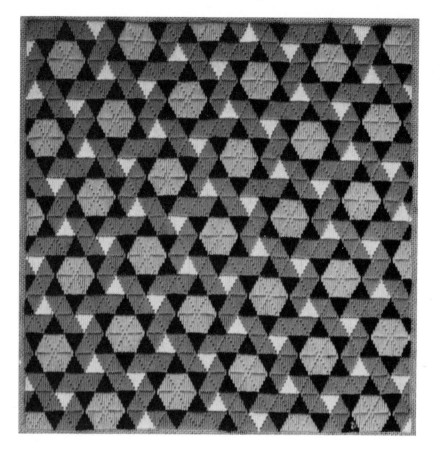

RIBBONED STARS

COLOR PLATE	39
CANVAS:	#16
YARN COLORS:	4
FINISHED SIZE:	13″ × 13″

Practical

1. Starting near top right, stitch the partially complete orange hexagon, then stitch the black triangle points of the star.
2. Stitch the blue rhombus forms that radiate from the black triangle points.
3. Directly below, and slightly to the left, stitch the next group of six black points, then stitch the orange hexagonal center, then the blue arms. Continue diagonally down to the next black-pointed star.
4. Return to the top, stitch the black-pointed orange star and the four blue arms that will complete the surround. Continue this in the diagonal descent established by the previous row.
5. After all the diagonal rows have been completed, fill in the white triangles.

Use

Pillows and, rescaled, floor cushion, wall hanging, table carpet. Black would be good for a border if one is desired. The black triangles and the white triangles can be exchanged as a variation.

Source

Seljuk brick pattern, 1067, Kharraqan tomb tower, western Iran. This tower has provided the book with a number of intriguing geometric designs (Color Plates and Sketchbook). I think it would be a fine idea to reunite them in yarn, in a related chromatic plan, for a group of pillows or floor cushions. Though their family tree may be known to the worker only, the kinship will establish a visual connection and rhythm.

VENETIAN TRIANGLES

Practical

The design consists of rows of triangles in two or three or four colors of yarn. The triangles of the first row are medium scarlet, deeper scarlet, black, and white. The triangles of the second row are marigold and green, those of the third, pale green, medium scarlet, deeper scarlet, and so forth. The rows should be worked horizontally, one at a time, and the Color Plate should be followed carefully.

Use

Pillow and, rescaled, wall hanging and floor cushion. This pattern breaks up into very varied optical effects, and its chameleon diversity, when viewed from different angles and distances, makes it a particularly good choice for a wall hanging (use #14 or #12 canvas and increase the number of stitches within the *triangle*). Simplicity of concept here produces a rich, variegated, refractive surface that would be equally at home in a drawing room, nursery, or office.

Source

Early medieval mosaic, San Marco Cathedral, Venice. Marigold yarn substitutes for real gold; otherwise the colors are the same. These can easily be changed, but the tonal values should be retained. You might like to do a series of pillows or floor cushions, in kindred colors, using the related patterns in Color Plate 41, or a large heraldic wall hanging incorporating them all.

COLOR PLATE	40
CANVAS:	#16
YARN COLORS:	7
FINISHED SIZE:	10″ × 10″

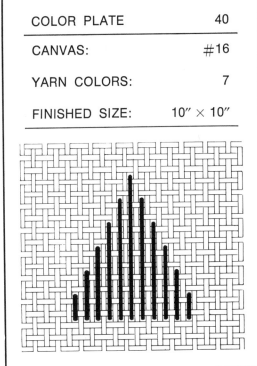

COLOR PLATE	41
CANVAS:	#16
YARN COLORS:	Various

Practical

All these patterns are related to the Venetian Triangles, Color Plate 40. Triangles and diamonds are placed in a simple arrangement across a given area to break up space. These triangles and diamonds are colored in a precise but uncomplicated repeating plan that offers no problem for the worker. Several needles, each threaded with one of the colors of the rows being executed, will be required.

Use

Pillows, floor cushions. I would like to see the patterns used for several mosaic pillows, or floor cushions, in identical or harmonizing colors. Rescaled larger, they can be assembled for a large, heraldic wall hanging. You can devise additional designs by exchanging tones (dark to light or vice versa) or colors, or you can experiment and create new ones. The shimmering mosaic surfaces of these patterns undergo considerable change when viewed from a slight distance or from various angles: their architecture becomes invisible, diamonds and triangles recede or disappear, and quite extraordinary designs emerge, changing once more as one moves about. This choreography is interesting but not disconcerting.

Source

Early medieval mosaics from the Cappella of San Pietro, Palermo, Sicily; the San Marco Cathedral, Venice; the Church of San Lorenzo, Rome. The colors have been changed, but the geometric and tonal architecture is very near the originals. They all require larger areas than those I provided, to establish their patterns and particular rhythms. (In a few of these patterns the angle of the triangle has been changed from the original.)

SPIRAL FLOWERS

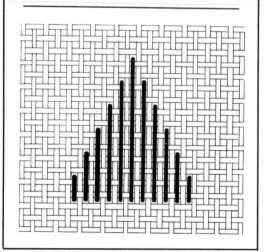

COLOR PLATE	42
CANVAS:	#16
YARN COLORS:	6
FINISHED SIZE:	13½″ × 15″

Practical

1. Start at upper right and complete the spiral arms (six) of one flower. Then complete all the spiral arms in diagonal rows.
2. Fill in the black background and the interiors of the flowers.
3. If working all the spiral arms first is confusing, work one flower at a time, filling in the blue stars and mustard half-hexagons as you proceed.

The route selected should be the most convenient for the traveler, and, indeed, you may wish to plot your own course for this or other designs. If a border is desired, the blue tones of the stars would be a good choice. The gold forms around the stars can be changed to very dark ginger brown. The medium ginger spiral arms will then look like tracery, and the effect is quite different.

Use

Floor cushion and table carpet. Use #18 canvas for a pillow, unless you prefer the large scale as shown.

Source

Original. The idea is loosely based on a field pattern in a nineteenth-century Turkoman carpet.

SAN MARCO LIGHTNING

Practical

1. Starting top right, work the first white zigzag row; this will establish the pattern.
2. Fill in at the top and then continue the horizontal zigzag rows.

Use

Floor cushion, wall hanging, table carpet. If more repeats or a smaller pillow are desired, #18 or #20 canvas should be used. The design suggests those frequently employed for flame stitch or Hungarian point (bargello); the 60-degree angle of trianglepoint imparts a curious three-dimensional relief when seen from a distance, and the trianglepoint architecture itself makes an interesting subsidiary pattern. Many other color combinations are possible; the pattern can be worked with great speed (use #14 canvas and more stitches in the *triangle* for a wall hanging). It is a good choice, because of its dignified strength (and fast results) for teen-agers to work on.

Source

Medieval mosaic, probably twelfth century, San Marco Cathedral, Venice. The colors are close to the original. Although the modern eye sees lightning or flames in these dynamic crags, my research makes me fairly certain that they were always and specifically employed to signify water. The design can be seen as a symbol for the sea, for irrigating canals, for floods, and probably for fecundity, in many artifacts of the Far and Middle East and medieval Europe.

COLOR PLATE	43
CANVAS:	#16
YARN COLORS:	4
FINISHED SIZE:	14¾″ × 15¼″

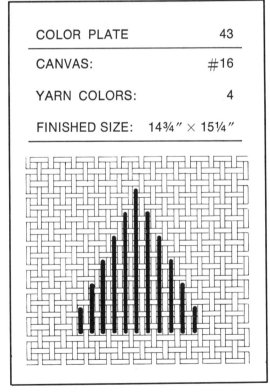

SAN MARCO STEPPED BOXES

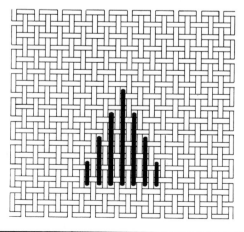

COLOR PLATE	44
CANVAS:	#14
YARN COLORS:	6
FINISHED SIZE:	13″ × 12″

Practical

1. Starting top right, stitch one horizontal zigzag row of the rhombus forms that make the sides of the "boxes" (two blues, one ginger).
2. Stitch the white diamond-shaped frames that lie immediately below the zigzag row. Stitch the zigzag row immediately below the white diamond frames, and continue, in the same fashion, to the end.
3. Fill in the light and dark gray triangles in the centers of the boxes.

Use

Pillow, floor cushion, and, rescaled larger, wall hanging or ceiling decoration. For a smaller pillow or for more repeats, #18 or #20 canvas should be used. The colors are close to the original and can be easily changed, provided you follow the tonal plan carefully.

Source

Medieval mosaic, San Marco Cathedral, Venice.

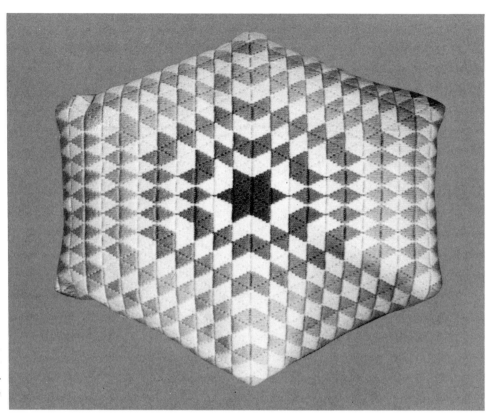

A group of small pillows in hexagonal shapes. They can be made larger by adding stitches to the *triangle*. Consult Color Plates and Work Pages. If preferred, rectangular surrounds can be stitched. See Color Plate 22.

7 Sketchbook

The drawings that follow are among the many visual notes made during the gathering-in phase of the book. I translated some into yarn (Color Plates), but a generous harvest meant relegating a large number to storage for future exploration. It seemed to me pointless to tuck them all away like private stock for a rainy day; it can't rain in my house, not for a while anyway, for I am anxious to re-resume my work on early Islamic carpets now twice interrupted—once, by my study of the square (*A Pageant of Pattern for Needlepoint Canvas*), and, again, by my involvement with the equilateral triangle. So, history and pattern monger that I am, they are offered here as ideas for projects, as additional homage to the Middle Eastern and Western artists who created most of them, and as further evidence of the unending fireworks that spark from the angles of this geometric form.

The diagram drawings are easy to understand and easy to use. Bear in mind that **every triangle** on the graph represents **one** *triangle* in needlework (or in fabric if the pattern is being used by quilters). Questions pertaining to scale, choice of materials, working techniques, and so forth should have been answered on the preceding pages devoted to these subjects. The drawings are shaded in strong contrasts for clarity. This can be either emphasized or tempered by the choice of yarn color. The designs in the Sketchbook can be paired harmoniously with those in the Color Plates, for they spring from related sources: pristine and modern; Middle Eastern, European, and American; brickwork, mosaics, miniature paintings, and patchwork quilts. They can be scaled to suit small or large articles, their tonal placement can be altered (interchanging darks, lights, and mediums) for unexpected metamorphoses, and borders or backgrounds can be added. All the working ideas applicable to the examples in the Color Plates, in other words, will be applicable to those in the Sketchbook. Turning the drawings on their sides or looking at them from various angles and distances can suggest ideas. Familiarity with the technique of trianglepoint (Chapter 4) will be helpful, of course.

Some suggestions for quilters will be found at the end of the chapter.

1. *Variations on a Theme*

The unshaded diagram, center, shows the linear foundation for surrounding patterns; many more can spring from the same source or from others of equally simple structure. Read the unshaded diagram from top right sloping diagonally to bottom left. It will be seen that the outlines, thus viewed, reveal a series of contiguously placed hexagons that are followed, in diagonal rows, by diamonds (rhombuses). These diamonds are always monotone in all but the diagram at top left. The patterning in these particular drawings arises from simple shading within the hexagons.

These patterns, plus others of your own devising, can be used in one patchwork piece for a wall hanging or floor cushion. Or they can be worked as individual pillows, large or small, in related colors and tones (blues and white; browns, beiges, and white). They will look like a series of mosaics if you use them for the floor. The eye may not perceive that they stem from the same ground, but the linear kinship by which they are governed will produce a rhythm that is as harmonious as it is mysterious.

2. *The Star of Bethlehem*

A favorite pattern of quilt collectors because it makes a vibrant, radiant wall hanging, this star really twinkles. Colors can be rearranged, of course, and the size can be altered by increasing or reducing the number of rhombuses that form the central hexagonal ground **before** the points are started. This will automatically enlarge or lessen the points themselves. This particular star design arrives courtesy of a Venetian kaleidoscope, and it is a fine specimen for a pillow, ceiling decoration, or wall hanging. See page 18 for a sophisticated and fascinating extension of this pattern as conceived and executed by a New York state quiltmaker in the early nineteenth century. You can duplicate this quilt, or part of it, by using this diagram as a start. It will make a large wall hanging or table carpet. Five shades or more.

3. The Flower Spiral

Diverse and intriguing patterns emerge from this design when it is viewed from different distances or angles (move the book around), making it an especially good choice for a wall hanging or a mosaic floor cushion. Work in a large scale as shown in Color Plate 27. The pattern might also be used as a center medallion for a telephone-directory cover or small pillow. Exchange the tonal values in the cubes for the back of the directory or for a companion pillow. Five shades.

4. Interlaced Star

This star has many antecedents: brick and tile arrangements still to be seen in many medieval Seljuk structures in Turkey and Persia; illustrations in curious alchemical and other mystical manuscripts; most familiarly as the Judaic Star of David or Seal of Solomon. Like the swastika (fylfot cross) it has had many uses, including an ancient one as a fertility symbol, the upward triangle representing male phallic power and the inverted triangle representing female womb-receptacle.

The lines of the small center star and those of the cubes in the border should be back-stitched. Four or more shades.

5. *Skewered S's*

If the S's are to be worked in monotone,
their outlines should be backstitched to
prevent their merging; alternatively, their
tone should be changed gently every other
row. Although this is my own design, S's
and Z's are to be met with in much ornamental work of the Middle Ages: in Islamic
architecture, tiles, embroideries, and carpets, in European textiles, mosaics, and in
illuminated manuscript decoration. There
are iconographic theories galore—the
snake as ancestral or medical deity, for
instance—none of which probably mat-
tered at all to the workers who undoubtedly
employed the motif for its ornamental
movement. Four or five shades.

6. *Quilt Hexagon*

This pattern, known to quilters as the
Hexagon, was favored during the nineteenth
century. Although it is an uncomplicated
counter-change, it is visually effective. The
unshaded area of the diagram shows the
basic structure. This can be worked in a
different color arrangement to form a border. Or the Hexagon pattern can be continued to whatever margins are chosen.
Two shades or more.

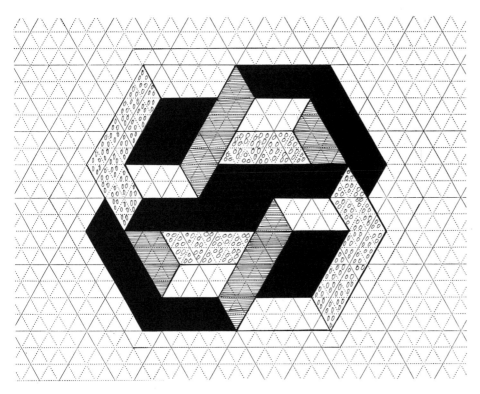

7. *Knotted Cube,* a., b., c.

a. One possible method for shading the design below right (b).

b. This design offers many opportunities for color experiment. It can be traced onto a piece of paper for color testing.

c. This is the negative of b., and it suggests the work of Albers. To achieve this in yarn, large *triangles* should be stitched in black so that the entire surface is covered. Then the cubic forms should be outlined in white yarn of the same or slightly lighter weight. This would make a fine pillow for a young person attracted to geometry or optics. The reverse side of the pillow might be stitched in opposite tones, light ground and black backstitch outline. The pattern should be rescaled if a wall hanging is desired.

119

8. *Prisms*

The inner construction and the coloring of these prismatic cubes can be altered in many ways. I have drawn all the steps so that alternatives may be easily considered. If the patterns are to be used together for a wall hanging (as shown), it is vital that the background color be in strong contrast to the cubes (see Color Plates 22, 23) and that the pattern be properly **scaled.** The bottom diagram shows one of the prisms rescaled for this purpose. These patterned prisms can also be used individually or as a group of hexagonally shaped pillows in different sizes but related colors. Three shades or more.

9. *Large Prism*

This can be worked in varied tones and colors. I suggest making the large center cube the darkest and graduating the surrounding cubes to mediums and lights, or vice versa, until the perimeter is reached. Jewel tones or golds, silvers, steels, or bronzes would sparkle well. Rescale larger for a crystalline wall hanging. It might be sensible to work out a color scheme on tracing paper before starting.

10. *Geometric Birds* a., b.

I call the dark forms "birds" because they so closely resemble the figures in the celebrated antique white-ground Turkish "bird" carpets to be found in the collections of museums and connoisseurs. The bird appellation is merely convenient to carpet scholars and dealers, and it is usually held that the figures really represent petals or foliage. But I think that these "birds" are based on an invisible geometric plan resembling that in diagram b. Diagrams a., c., and d. (see following page) are my own adaptations of diagram b.

b. This is adapted from a small brick motif in the Kharraqan tomb tower, Seljuk-Turkish eleventh century, Iran. I would like to see these patterns used individually for pillows in various hexagonal shapes, and in shades of Chinese or Delft blue and white. The diagram at the foot of b. is the unshaded outline of the pattern used in diagram a.

10. *Geometric Birds* c., d.

11. *Turkish and Persian Borders* a., b., c.

a. This is based on a brick pattern in the Kharraqan tomb tower, Seljuk-Turkish, eleventh century, western Iran.

b. From the Persian miniature painting, "A Convivial Gathering," c. 1590, Chester Beatty Library, Dublin.

c. From a portal border in a Turkish miniature painting, "The Circumcision of Shehzade Bayazid," fifteenth century, Topkapi Saray Museum, Istanbul. Note the resemblance to Egyptian Hexapod, Color Plate 13.

All three patterns can be continued to form all-over field designs.

12. *Links and Chains* a., b., c.

a. This is a strong field pattern composed of diagonal "links," and it would be handsome in golds or bronzes on dark steel. The outlines of the links can be backstitched in fine yarn for clear delineation.

b. and c. These are border patterns from a sixteenth-century Persian miniature painting and can be used in alternate rows or in another arrangement for a pillow design.

13. *Turkish Starred Wheels*

This is adapted from a brick motif in the thirteenth-century Seljuk-Turkish building, Konya. It is also to be found as a carpet field pattern in a sixteenth-century Turkish miniature painting, "The Reception of the King of Erdel," Topkapi Saray Museum, Istanbul, and as a tile pattern in a Persian miniature painting, "Life in the City" from *The Khamsa of Nizami,* sixteenth-century, the Fogg Art Museum, Boston.

See Color Plate 32.

14. *Persian Starred Wheels*

This was adapted from a sixteenth-century Persian miniature painting. Its resemblance to the preceding design is obvious, but its rhythm and effect are quite different. The stars' color can be changed in alternate rows. Both 13 and 14 are fairly large-scale designs that can be used for wall hangings, ceiling decorations, floor pillows, table carpets. If used as the latter, a border design can be borrowed from one of the Color Plates or a solid surround can provide the border. Three or more shades.

See Color Plate 32.

15. *Sirçali Patterns* a., b., c.

These designs are all from the Sirçali *medrese,* 1243, Seljuk-Turkish, Konya. The building contains many mihrab (pointed arch) shaped niches as part of its ornamental structure, each one further enhanced by geometric tile designs, some of which are based on the square, some on the pentagon, and some on the equilateral triangle—hexagon. These diagrams are, of course, based on the last.

  a. Sirçali Arrowheads
  b. Sirçali Zigzag
  c. Sirçali Rhombus

16. *Sirçali X*

Another design from the generous Sirçali *medrese.* In the original the small triangles, set above and below the hexagons, are white. Three shades.

17. *Seljuk Arrowheads*

This pattern, and others that are closely related, can be found in brick on thirteenth- and fourteenth-century buildings in Konya and other Seljuk centers in Turkey and Persia. It is a pleasing all-over design that can be used for pillows and floor cushions —and even for a hanging if you wish to add an architectural ornament to your wall. Three shades.

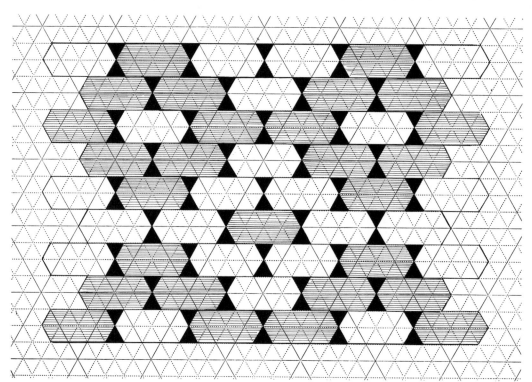

18. *Persian Brick*

This is adapted from a brick mausoleum, 1304–1313. It is the only building still in existence in the extinct Persian city of Sultaniya. The pattern is suitable in scale for a wall hanging only. The "bricks" will have to be shaded or backstitched to keep their outlines distinct and separate from one another. Three shades.

19. *Persian Knots* a., b.

a. A "knotted" hexagon taken from a carpet pattern in a sixteenth-century Persian miniature painting.

b. A variation of Color Plates 14, 15. These "knots" require backstitched outlines to clarify their form. See aforementioned Color Plates. Three shades.

20. *Diagonal Scallops,* a., b.

a. This is a pattern from the Cappella of San Pietro, Palermo, Sicily, which houses a most extraordinary collection of twelfth-century Norman–Moorish geometric mosaics. A composition that grows in interest and subtle metamorphoses the longer one regards it. Its cousin, Palermo Meander, Color Plate 20, is equally intriguing. Three shades.

b. Diagonal Scallops Variation.

21. *San Marco Boxes*

This is taken from another building that glows with early medieval geometric splendors, the San Marco Cathedral in Venice. The mosaics from which this is derived are said to date from the eleventh or twelfth century. A large-scale pattern, it is most suitable for a wall hanging unless worked on an 18- or 20-squares-to-the-inch canvas. It is interesting turned on its side. Four shades.

22. *Tiered Cubes*

Another medieval mosaic from the San Marco Cathedral, Venice. This pattern looks quite different when turned on its side. Four shades.

23. *French Z's* a., b.

a. The pattern on the field of the drawing is from a French medieval mosaic. It can also be extended beyond the hexagon to form a rectangular-shaped pillow, if preferred. Five shades.

b. *French Z's Variation*

The Z's are here intercepted by diamond forms in vertical rows, and the result is a very different pattern. Three shades.

24. *Roman Mosaics* a., b.

These patterns are adapted from thirteenth-century mosaics in the church of Santa Maria Maggiore, Rome, but they look very much like the forms we see in Florentine flame stitch embroidery; they would certainly lend themselves to similar subtle shading methods. The originals, or at least the reproductions of the originals I saw in an early-nineteenth-century illustration, were in brown, golden-beige, and white. Three shades.

25. *Miscellany* a., b.

Diagrams a. and b. show how minute alterations in coloring can be applied to the same linear ground plan for different patterns. These are also interesting turned on their sides. Diagrams c. and d. are examples of the same on another ground structure.

Diagram e. is a counterchange pattern that can be additionally divided, as shown in the various "urn" forms. They can be worked in simple two-tone as shown, or the dark "urn" can be divided, or the light, or both.

Diagram f. is a variation of Color Plate 12. The cubes can be worked in graduated tones of one color, or each cube can change its color (also in graduated tones). The cubes must be constructed in triangles of fewer stitches than those in the color plate to allow space for the pattern to repeat itself.

Diagram g. is a simple cube construction that might be made by children for a small wall hanging. The three sides of the individual cubes must be made in different tones or colors so that the "boxes" or "dice" do not merge.

133

25. *Miscellany* c., d.

25. *Miscellany* e., f., g.

MATERIALS

The Canvas

All details relating to canvas, such as gauge, appropriate functions, yarns, color, are examined thoroughly under Rescaling, pages 24–26. The raw edges of canvas, after cutting, will have to be taped or sewed to stop raveling.

It is advisable, as with all handwork, to use the best materials that are available and still within your budget. It is spendthrift to waste hours of good labor on unworthy materials that will offer little pleasure in the course of work and that will eventually fall victim to the ravages of your own dislike, as well as to those of time and wear.

Yarn

Most of the designs in this book have a glossy, luminous quality, and the warmth of the wool provides a valuable counterbalance to this and to the geometric composition. But it is vital that this clean geometry and smooth surface not be marred or disturbed by a discordant, thick outline backstitched in fat, vulgar yarn. Any yarn commonly employed for needlepoint work is suitable for trianglepoint if it covers the canvas well without bulking. In this respect, yarns that can be split, such as the Persian (now manufactured and obtainable in a number of countries) and Nantucket worsted, are the most versatile, for their thickness or weight can always be adjusted by the removal or addition of one or more of the separable strands. Persian-type yarns are available in most U.S. shops that sell needlepoint supplies. I did not use them for the book, as much as I like and respect them, because their filaments become too feathery when photographic enlargements are required. I also very much like the glossy, smooth texture of tapestry yarns. And the mirror gleam of silk on #18 or #20 canvas is most appropriate to these mosaic designs.

There are times when an essential shade or quality of tone cannot be found within the range of the particular brand being used. Rather than compromise, seek the color elsewhere. Many of these designs were worked in the sunny, clear tones of Nantucket worsted, many in the fine, patrician colors of Laine Colbert or Appleton tapestry wools, and, when necessary, I used all three together, perhaps a blue of one, a green of another, a red of another —combining the products of the United States, France, and England. In no circumstances should yarns or colors be blended in the needle itself. No matter how urgent your need, the eye of the needle is no place for a wedding; the textures and tones, despite your efforts, will remain stubbornly independent. For specifics about relating yarns to canvas, and the reverse, please consult the chapter Trianglepoint Basics, Rescaling Method Three. There are many other brands of tapestry yarns available in shops—such as D.M.C. Laine Tapisserie—that would also be well suited to this work.

The Needle

The tapestry needle with the blunt tip and long eye, commonly employed for needlepoint work, can be found in different sizes in all shops dealing with embroidery or counted canvas work. The needle selected should have an eye large enough to allow the free movement of yarn, without abrasion or crushing, and it should be small enough not to dislodge the threads of the canvas as it travels through the holes. I find #18 or #20 a good all-purpose size. A finer needle must be kept on hand for the backstitching. Backstitching should be handled with precision and delicacy, and with as little disturbance as possible to the stitches of the *triangles*. Intensely concentrated workers sometimes find that the acid produced by the hand roughens and darkens the needle. Fine sandpaper or a soapy steel-wool wash will restore cleanliness and smoothness. A discolored needle will affect the color of the yarn, and its roughened surface will retard the smooth glide of your stitching, slowing your progress. In fact, this last will be your signal that something is amiss and that your needle needs your attention. Try to attend to it quickly.

The Marker

Some workers like to mark their canvases with a vertical line running down the center of the canvas and a horizontal line running across the center of the canvas, thus quartering the work area and keeping the centering lines in view throughout the working. Trianglepoint rarely requires this, but with new designs or unfamiliar variations it is sometimes advisable. In this case fold the canvas in half vertically, then fold it in half horizontally, and mark the center juncture point with a dot. Draw four lines radiating out from this center dot, making certain not to rail-jump as you draw between or on threads. Use **waterproof, permanent, indelible** medium gray markers, tipped with extra-fine nibs. Three adjectives because one or more always appears on the label, but all should be considered guilty until proved innocent. Test the marker each time you buy a new one—**even** when it is a seeming twin of one you have found to be reliable. Draw some lines on paper or fabric, allow them to dry, immerse the paper or fabric in cool water, stare. If you see any evidence at all of blurring, any hint of bleeding dyes, return the marker to the store with evidence in hand and ask for your money to be returned. I can almost assure you of dissatisfaction; the store will not oblige; but I think false claims are false claims and should be so labeled. India ink is preferred by many professionals for this sort of drawing, and it has always been regarded as the most dependable medium for such work. But we live in interesting times, and I had a complicated wall hanging very nearly destroyed by an "indelible" India ink that ran shamelessly. The marking liquid **must** be absolutely waterproof or it will discolor the yarn during the blocking process.

SUPPLIERS

UNITED STATES

Yarns and Canvas

Many shops and department stores throughout the United States and Canada supply needlepoint materials. If you cannot find what you require in your area, information about local stores can be obtained from the distributors below.

American Crewel and Canvas Studio, P.O. Box 298, Boonton, N.J. 07005.
Appleton tapestry yarn, Appleton crewel yarn, canvas.
The D M C Corporation, 107 Trumbull Avenue, Elizabeth, N.J. 07206.
Laine tapisserie.
Handwork Tapestries, P.O. Box 54, Baldwin, New York.
Laine Colbert tapestry yarn, Médicis yarn, Colbert 6 Persian yarn, Au Vers à Soie French silk yarn, canvas.
Joan Toggitt, Ltd., 1170 Broadway, New York, N.Y. 10001.
Appleton tapestry yarn, Appleton crewel yarn, canvas.
C. R. Meissner Co., Inc., 22 East 29th Street, New York, N.Y. 10016.

Laine Colbert tapestry yarn, Paternayan Persian yarn, Au Vers à Soie French silk yarn, Médicis yarn, canvas.

Nantucket Needleworks, 11 South Water Street, Nantucket, Mass. 02554.
    Nantucket worsted yarn, canvas.

Paternayan Bros., Inc., 312 East 95th Street, New York, N.Y. 10028.
    Paternayan Persian yarn, canvas.

Scandinavian Art Handicraft, 7696 Camargo Road, Madeira, Cincinnati, Ohio 45243.
    Au Vers à Soie French silk yarn.

Isometric Graph Paper

The Keuffel and Esser Company, 40 East 43rd Street, New York, N.Y., 10017, for New York city residents; all other inquiries should be made to 20 Whippany Road, Morristown, N.J., 07960. Order number 46 4231. Order by sheet or in bulk. Also address inquiries about local suppliers to the New Jersey office.

SUPPLIERS

GREAT BRITAIN

Yarns and Canvas

Supplies can be ordered through the post from the following addresses.

Mrs Mary Allen, Turnditch, Derbyshire

Beecrafts, 77 Church Street, Guisborough, Cleveland

The Campden Needlecraft Centre, High Street, Chipping Campden, Gloucestershire

B. Francis, 4 Glentworth Street, London NW 1

The Handworkers' Market, 8 Fish Street, Holt, Norfolk

The Ladies Work Society Ltd, Delabere House, Moreton-in-Marsh, Gloucestershire

Mace & Nairn, 89 Crane Street, Salisbury, Wiltshire

The Needlewoman, 146 Regent Street, London W1

Christine Riley, 53 Barclay Street, Stonehaven, Kincardineshire

The Royal School of Needlework, 25 Princes Gate, London SW 7

Mrs Joan L. Trickett, 110 Marsden Road, Burnley, Lancashire

Mrs J. Whittington, Park Cottage, Brampton Bryan, Bucknell, Shropshire

Mrs A. M. Wilson, 135 Hall Drive, Middlesbrough, Cleveland

Yarns, 37 High Street, Wellington, Somerset

Isometric Graph Paper

Isometric graph paper can be ordered through the post, by the pad, from U. D. O., 23 Bloomsbury Way, London WC 1

9 A Note to Quilters

The architecture of trianglepoint needlework, unlike other stitching systems used on the counted canvas, is one that is both practical and fertile for quilt artisans. Please consult Color Plate 5 and the corresponding Work Page. All the designs in the book have a like construction. Each *triangle* in the design is a monochromatic entity not unlike a fabric cutout or mosaic piece. The *triangle* is always uniform throughout the design; it never changes size. The designs evolve from the placement and juxtaposition of *triangles* of diverse colors, just as in pieced patchwork. Not only are they ideally suited in structural form, scale, tonal arrangement, and pattern to the technique of the pieced patchwork quilt (which is the technique of mosaic work adapted from the tesserae to the fabric), but most of the designs will be new and fresh to the field. For this reason, both the Color Plates and the Sketchbook can be used as sources. The modern optical cubes in the Color Plates and Sketchbook should be of particular interest to those who would like to move in new directions, and the examples comprising Persian miniatures, Seljuk architectural bricks and tiles, Venetian and Sicilian–Norman–Moorish mosaics will be as enthralling in fabric as in their original mediums. The patterns that brought such kaleidoscopic splendors to the Persian and Turkish palaces and pavilions can be recycled into patchwork with much the same effect (see page opposite). A few designs are made with a backstitched outline. This presents a problem for the quilter, but perhaps it is one that can be solved.

Persian miniature painting, "Life in the City," c. 1540. The Fogg Art Museum, Harvard University. Daily doings in the palace—and considerable hexagonal activity, too.

139

Bibliography

Aslanapa, Oktay, *Turkish Art and Architecture.* New York: Praeger, 1971

Bentley, W. A., and Humphreys, W. J., *Snow Crystals,* revised edition. New York: Dover Publications, Inc., 1962

von Bode, Wilhelm, and Kühnel, Ernst, *Antique Rugs from the Near East.* London: G. Bell and Sons, 1970

Boito, Camillo, ed., *La Basilica di San Marco in Venezia Illustrata nella Storia e nel'Arte da Scrittore Veneziana.* Venice: F. Ongania, 1880–1888

Christie, Archibald H., *Pattern Design.* New York: Dover Publications, Inc., 1969

Colby, Averil, *Patchwork Quilts.* New York: Charles Scribner's Sons, 1965

Dimand, Maurice, and Grube, Ernst J., *The Khamsa of Nizami.* New York: The Metropolitan Museum of Art, 1969

Erdmann, Kurt, *Europa und Der Orientteppich.* Berlin: Florian Kupferberg, 1962

————, *Seven Hundred Years of Oriental Carpets.* London: Faber and Faber, 1970. American Edition: University of California Press, Berkeley, 1970

Evans, J., ed., *The Flowering of the Middle Ages.* New York: McGraw-Hill, 1966. London: Thames and Hudson, 1966

Finley, Ruth, *Old Patchwork Quilts and the Women Who Made Them.* Newton Center, Mass.: Chas. T. Branford Co., 1971

Grube, Ernst J., *The World of Islam.* London: Paul Hamlyn Ltd., 1966

Hall, Carrie, and Kretsinger, Rose G., *The Romance of the Patchwork Quilt.* New York: Bonanza Books, 1935

Hill, Derek, and Grabar, Oleg, *Islamic Architecture and Its Decoration.* London: Faber and Faber, Ltd., 1964

Holstein, Jonathan, *The Pieced Quilt.* New York: New York Graphic Society, 1973

Hornung, Clarence, *Handbook of Designs and Devices,* revised edition. New York: Dover Publications, Inc., 1959

Jones, Owen, *Grammar of Ornament.* London: Day and Son, 1856

Lantz, Sherlee, *A Pageant of Pattern for Needlepoint Canvas.* New York: Atheneum, 1973; new edition, Grosset & Dunlap, Inc., 1975. London: Andre Deutsch, 1973

Panofsky, Erwin, *Early Netherlandish Painting,* vols. 1 and 2. Cambridge: Harvard University Press, 1953; paper edition, vol. 2. New York: Harper and Row, 1974

Racinet, Albert Charles Auguste, *L'Ornament Polychrome.* Paris: Firmin Didot et Cie, 1885

Rice, David Talbot, *Islamic Art.* London: Thames and Hudson, 1965

Robinson, B. W., *Persian Miniature Painting.* London: The Victoria and Albert Museum, 1967

Spies, Werner, *Albers.* New York: Harry N. Abrams, Inc., 1971

Terzi, Andrea, *La Cappella di San Pietro nella Reggia di Palermo.* Palermo: A. Brangi, 1889

von Wersin, Wolfgang, *Das Elementare Ornament.* Ravensburg: Otto Maier Verlag, 1940

Index

Figures in italic type indicate the numbers of the Color Plates or Sketchbook Diagrams. Figures following indicate the page numbers on which the Color Plates or Sketchbook Diagrams appear.